OVID
METAMORPHOSES III

EDITED WITH INTRODUCTION,
NOTES AND VOCABULARY
BY A.A.R. HENDERSON
LECTURER IN HUMANITY AT THE UNIVERSITY OF GLASGOW

PUBLISHED BY BRISTOL CLASSICAL PRESS
GENERAL EDITOR: JOHN H. BETTS

Cover illustration: A maenad (follower of Dionysus), holding in her right hand a **thyrus** with ivy leaves and in her left a small panther or leopard; she has the skin of a similar animal tied about her neck and her hair bound around with a snake. From the white-ground interior of an early fifth-century BC wine-cup (**cylix**) of the Athenian red-figure style by the so-called Brygos painter; **Antikensammlungen, Munich**. [Drawing by Jean Bees]

First published in 1979
New impression with minor corrections and revisions published in 1981 by
Bristol Classical Press
an imprint of
Gerald Duckworth & Co. Ltd
The Old Piano Factory
48 Hoxton Square, London N1 6PB

Reprinted 1991, 1994, 1995

A catalogue record for this book is available
from the British Library

ISBN 0-906515-02-5

Available in USA and Canada from:
Focus Information Group
PO Box 369
Newburyport
MA 01950

Printed in Great Britain by
Booksprint, Bristol

CONTENTS

FOR CLARE

FOREWORD

No English commentary on Book 3 has been published since that by Miss M. Cartwright (Oxford, 1909), which has long been out of print and is now, in any case, unsatisfactory. (For example, the story of Semele is omitted as 'unsuitable'.) Book 3 offers the sixth-form pupil and first year University student a marvellous introduction, via some of the best-known myths of ancient Greece, to the enchanted, often violent, often sad, often funny world of the *Metamorphoses*. Not only does it possess a homogeneity unusual among the poem's fifteen books, following as it does (with one major digression) the fortunes of the founders of the Theban royal house and aristocracy, but also the stories in it are related at length, which allows the reader time to savour the individual quality of each episode and to fix its *dramatis personae* in mind and memory. This can be a problem in other books, where story presses hungrily upon story and a bewildering gallery of characters, human and divine, passes before the eye.

This is a simple and utilitarian edition. The Introduction contains nothing new or controversial, attempts no systematic criticism of the poem, has nothing to say on the influence of the *Metamorphoses* on later literatures, but tries to place it in its ancient context and help the young scholar to approach it with some degree of understanding. The Notes aim first and foremost at aiding comprehension of the Latin. To this end they offer grammatical and syntactical explanation of a kind which my own recent experience suggests is most necessary (case-usage, for instance, receives a good deal of attention). At the same time the aesthetic and antiquarian aspects are given, it is hoped, adequate coverage. After some debate a Vocabulary has also been included. This started out as Miss Cartwright's, but so many omissions have had to be filled and inaccuracies corrected that it amounts to a new one.

Although I have sought to take a fresh and independent view of the text, it would have been foolish not to make extensive use of Franz Bömer's commentary. I must acknowledge a debt to him in several points of interpretation, as well as for supplying quite a few of the parallel passages that are quoted. My debt to certain of the items listed in the Bibliography will be apparent to anyone familiar with them; I extend my thanks to the authors concerned. I am grateful to Professor Niall Rudd of Bristol for reading the typescript and making a number of helpful suggestions, and also to the General Editor for his advice, encouragement, co-operation and patience.

Glasgow,
20 March 1979
(*die natali Nasonis, anno post poetam natum MMXXI*)

In this, the edition's second impression some
corrections have been made to misprints and a number
of minor revisions have been incorporated. Several
of the latter have been included as a result of
comments by Mr J. D. Christie, Professor P. G. Walsh
and Dr. F. J. Williams and I am grateful for their
constructive criticisms.

Glasgow   A.A.R.H.
29 July 1981

INTRODUCTION

1. *THE POET*.

Publius Ovidius Naso ('Ovid' to us, but 'Naso' to
the Romans) was born on 20th March, 43 B.C. at Sulmo
(modern Sulmona), a small *municipium* some 80 miles east
of Rome near Corfinium. He came from an old 'county'
family of native Paelignian stock, enfranchised before
the Social War, which had long enjoyed equestrian status.
For his secondary schooling he was sent with his elder
brother to Rome, where he studied rhetoric under Arellius
Fuscus and M. Porcius Latro. After spending some time in
Athens he went on the customary 'Grand Tour' of the Greek
world, visiting Ionia (including the ruins of Troy) and
Sicily. On his return he took the first steps towards
a senatorial career by serving in junior magistracies,
first as one of the *tresviri capitales* in charge of pri-
sons and executions, then on the panel of the *decemviri
stlitibus iudicandis*, who presided over the centumviral
court. But he soon decided to retire into private life
in order to write. He had given the first reading from
his poems while still in his 'teens (c. 26 B.C.), at the
instigation of his patron M. Valerius Messalla Corvinus,
and was already friendly or at least acquainted with Propertius, Tibullus and Horace (though not Virgil). With
the publication of the first book of the *Amores* he leapt
into prominence as a poet of love. Four more books followed, and his reputation was sealed by the *Ars Amatoria*
and *Remedia Amoris*.

Ovid was married three times, first as a mere youth
to a girl who was 'neither suitable nor useful', secondly
to a 'blameless' (but dull?) lady who bore him a daughter,
thirdly to a well-connected widow with a girl of her own.
This last marriage was a happy and enduring one. In his
fiftieth year (8 A.D.), while putting the finishing touches
to the *Metamorphoses* and perhaps the *Fasti* too, he was
suddenly ordered by Augustus to leave Italy and go into
exile at Tomis, a primitive frontier town on the Black
Sea (present-day Constanza in Romania). He himself says
only that 'a poem and a mistake' caused his downfall, and
that the mistake consisted in seeing, not doing, something
criminal. The poem in question was the *Ars Amatoria*, which
he tried to defend in Book 2 of the *Tristia*. What the of-
fence was nobody knows, although many theories have been
advanced, such as that Ovid was implicated in a plot against
Augustus involving Julia, granddaughter of the *princeps*,
or that he secretly and sacrilegiously attended the rites
of the Bona Dea, whose worship was restricted to women.
Although he strove to have his sentence terminated, by

writing verse epistles to his wife and friends in Rome
(the *Tristia* and *Epistulae ex Ponto*), neither Augustus
nor his successor Tiberius relented. After some eight
years' exile Ovid died in late 17 or early 18 A.D. among
the inhumani Getae, in whose barbaric tongue he claimed
to have written a poem - in praise of Augustus. The epi-
taph he composed for himself (*Tristia* 3.3.73 - 6) today
graces his statue in Constanza:

> Hic ego, qui iaceo, tenerorum lusor amorum,
>   ingenio perii Naso poeta meo.
> at tibi qui transis, ne sit grave, quisquis amasti,
>   dicere: 'Nasonis molliter ossa cubent.'

About Ovid's personal appearance we have no information whatever. Seneca (*Controversiae* 2.2.8) describes
him as having a 'refined, upright and likeable nature'
('comptum et decens et amabile ingenium'), which is at
least not wildly at odds with the impression one gains
from reading his work, particularly the autobiographical
poems of his exile, where there is no *persona* to sustain.
These afford many details of his habits and likes and dis-
likes - e.g. he was a keen gardener, had no time for gambl-
ing, and drank very little - which are of interest, without
having any bearing on his poetry. Very full accounts of
Ovid the man are provided by L. P. Wilkinson in *Ovid Recalled* (chapters 1 and 9) and by A. G. Lee in the Introduction to his excellent Pitt Press edition of *Metamorphoses* 1.

2. THE POEM

The *Metamorphoses* occupied Ovid for some eight years
prior to his banishment. It is his only poem in hexameters,
and the largest and most ambitious of all his works (fifteen books, 12,000 lines). His previous output consisted
almost exclusively of elegiac verse: *Amores* (five - later
abridged to three - books), about a (fictitious affair
with a woman called Corinna; *Epistulae Heroidum* or *Heroides*,
love letters from lonely women of mythology to their men-
folk (1 - 15) supplemented by three pairs of letters between
lovers (16 - 21), e.g. Paris to Helen and her reply; *Medi-
camina Faciei Femineae*, a frivolous didactic piece on cos-
metics (lines 1 - 100 survive); *Ars Amatoria* (three books,
1 and 2 addressed to men, 3 to women), on the techniques of
courtship and seduction, with Ovid in the role of instruc-
tor; and *Remedia Amoris*, an equally unserious textbook on
ending a liaison should the other party prove unsatisfactory.

He had also written a tragedy, *Medea*, which won high praise but is now lost. This was the only *maius opus*; all the rest were light verse. But the *Medea* was a youthful composition, and anyway tragedy, for the Augustans as for the Alexandrians, was a 'fringe' genre (Ovid's play, like those of Seneca later, was intended for reading, not acting). By his forties he was looking for bigger worlds to conquer. Epic, which had made a magnificent comeback in the shape of Virgil's *Aeneid* (published in 17 B.C.), was uncongenial to him. He was attracted by mythology and antiquarian matters but his literary sympathies lay with the Alexandrian school of Callimachus, who had come down strongly against epic poetry. Callimachus' own *Aetia* suggested a similar work on a Roman subject, and so was conceived the *Fasti*, an aetiological poem relating the 'causes' (*causae*, αἰτια) or origins of the various festivals of the Roman religious calendar. Out of a projected twelve books, six are extant (January to June); complete, it would have reached about 10,000 lines. Simultaneously, it seems, Ovid hit upon the idea of the *Metamorphoses*, though its genesis was more complex.

He announces the poem in a singularly brief yet densely packed prologue (1.1 - 4), as follows:

In nova fert animus mutatas dicere formas
corpora. di, coeptis (nam vos mutastis et illa)*
aspirate meis, primaque ab origine mundi
ad mea perpetuum deducite tempora carmen.

This tells the reader four things: (1) the work he is about to embark on is something entirely new: in nova fert animus can - and is meant to - make an independent sentence; a listener will pick this up more readily than a reader, whose eye is already running ahead, 'transforming' the syntax into statement (2) ; (2) its theme is transformations (formas in nova corpora mutatas); (3) its limits are Creation at one end (prima origo mundi) and Ovid's own day at the other (mea tempora); (4) it is in form a carmen perpetuum or continuous poem.

Ovid's claim of originality does not refer to subject matter. Transformations were not a new topic for either prose or poetry. Both Homer and Hesiod show familiarity with the phenomenon, e.g. the metamorphosis of Mestra in Hesiod's *Catalogue of Women* (Merkelbach-West, fragments 43 - 5), on which Ovid draws in 8.739 ff. There are also fragments of satyr-plays by Sophocles (*Inachus*) and Euripides that depict Io's changing into a heifer and

---

* illa (a correction by P. Lejay of the Mss.' illas) is certainly right.

Cadmus' into a snake respectively, passages evidently
known to Ovid (1.738 ff. and 4.583 ff.). The *Argonautica*
of Apollonius Rhodius contains (3.138 ff.) a famous scene
in which Jason kills the earthborn men, whose varying
stages of development are described; this too is adapted
by Ovid (3.106 ff.; see Notes *ad loc.*). A certain Boeus
(or Boeo) wrote a poem about birds which had once been
people, the *Ornithogonia* (? c.275 B.C.), which in Ovid's
youth his friend Aemilius Macer translated into Latin;
and later in the 3rd century B.C. the astronomer Eratosthenes brought out a prose collection of stories about
human beings who became stars, the *Catasterismi*. The
first poem about metamorphoses in general was the 2nd
century poet Nicander's *Heteroeumena* in five books, which
Ovid is known to have consulted. Nearer his own day Par-
thenius of Nicaea (who is said to have taught Virgil
Greek) published a *Metamorphoses* which was perhaps a med-
ley of prose and verse, and a certain Theodorus, otherwise
unknown, wrote a prose work under the same title. Both
of these Ovid used. Dictionaries of mythology were also
available, such as the *Bibliotheca* of Apollodorus (the
work of that name extant today, often cited in the Notes,
is a post-Ovidian compilation), and the odd handbook.
Everything (except Macer's translation) was of course in
Greek. So Ovid could justifiably claim to be breaking
new ground by introducing the metamorphosis-poem into
Latin. But the originality of his *Metamorphoses* goes
much deeper than that.

Ovid makes a point of describing it as a *carmen perpetuum*. The phrase plainly recalls the ἓν ἄεισμα διηνεκές
('one continuous song') against which Callimachus inveighed
in the Prologue to the *Aetia* (Pfeiffer, fragment 1). So
the question arises whether Ovid is meeting Callimachus
head on (which would seem unlikely), or whether he is
using *carmen perpetuum* in a rather different sense. Hollis,
in the Introduction (p. xii) of his edition of *Metamorphoses* 8, argues that while Callimachus is objecting to
narrative continuity, Ovid is claiming chronological continuity (i.e. he will omit no period of time between
Creation and his own day). But this is not altogether
plausible; for Ovid takes great care to secure *perpetuitas*
of narrative and is not worried about maintaining a clear-
cut chronological progression. It seems more likely that,
whereas Callimachus had in mind a long continuous poem
telling one main story, Ovid was introducing a long continuous poem with many different stories. So although
the *Metamorphoses* did not have the thematic unity of
traditional epic (nor the homogeneity of its heroic spirit), it could still claim to be a continuous poem rather
than a mere sequence of tales.

This continuity is achieved in two related ways. The first is by constructing patterns of stories within stories, the second by engineering ingenious and unobtrusive transitions between them. This kind of internal patterning is a characteristic of the epyllion or 'little epic', which Callimachus encouraged as a substitute for the full-blown epic, in particular the so-called 'inset' epyllion, exemplified by Callimachus' own *Hecale* (fragments 230 - 376), in which the tale of Erysicthon is enclosed within the main tale of Theseus and the Bull of Marathon, by his fifth *Hymn*, in which *Artemis and Actaeon* is inset within *Pallas and Tiresias,* or later by Moschus' *Europa* in which the transformation of Io, one of Zeus' (Jupiter's) illicit loves, into a cow is enclosed within the rape of Europa in which Zeus assumes the form of a bull to pursue another amour. The non-inset epyllion, such as Theocritus 13 (*Hylas*) or 24 (*Heracliscus*), is far less important as a *structural* model for the *Metamorphoses*.

In the first century B.C. Latin poets of the Neoteric school had already written epyllia. The sole survivor is Catullus 64, in which *Theseus and Ariadne* makes a digression inside *Peleus and Thetis*. Many other titles exist, but we cannot say with confidence whether they were inset or not; e.g. the *Io* of Calvus (from which Ovid adapted a line - 1.632), the *Zmyrna* (*Myrrha*) of Cinna, the *Glaucus* of Cornificius, the *Alcyone* of Cicero - all of which have transformation as their theme. Virgil however composed an inset epyllion, *Aristaeus* enclosing *Orpheus and Eurydice,* for the end of the *Georgics* (4.315 ff.), and we may guess that the majority of Neoteric epyllia were inset. The length of an Alexandrine epyllion varied (Eratosthenes' *Hermes* had c. 1,600 lines, Catullus 64 has 408). Ovid works with both shorter and longer units, single and double inset. Thus in 2.531 - 632 *Apollo and Coronis* encloses *Neptune and Corone,* a quite short single inset; whereas in 1.568 - 747 the story of Io encloses that of Syrinx, related to Argus by Mercury, a longer unit in which the scheme is a double inset:- A_1 (*Io*) - B_1 (*Argus*) - C (*Syrinx*) - B_2 (*Argus*) - A_2 (*Io*). Book 3 shows an inset epyllion in *Pentheus* (containing *Acoetes' Tale*), and a case can be made for regarding *Tiresias* and *Narcissus* and *Echo* as exhibiting the form of a double inset (*Tiresias - Echo - Narcissus - Echo - Tiresias*), since Tiresias reappears after Narcissus' death, as does Echo a little before him. But the tales of Echo and Narcissus are so intertwined that it is best not to tease them apart for formal purposes, and furthermore Tiresias' transformation (into a woman, and back again) occurs *before* the tale of Echo and Narcissus.

However the whole of Book 3 forms part of a vast pattern
extending from 3.1 to 4.603, which we may call *The Family
of Cadmus*. *Cadmus*, at the start of Book 3, is not com-
pleted until 4.563 ff., when Cadmus and Harmonia change
into snakes. For after *Pentheus* comes another inset epyllion, *The Daughters of Minyas* (4.1 - 415), enclosing a
sequence of three stories (*Pyramus and Thisbe*, *Clytie
and Leucothoe*, *Salmacis and Hermaphroditus*); lastly comes
Ino (416 - 562) before Cadmus' eventual reappearance.

Ovid's technique, then (and there are still more
complex examples elsewhere in the poem), is to combine
tales into epyllion-type groups, and to build up the
work from these blocks. This has two great advantages:
it removes the need for continual chronological pointers
by substituting a much more cogent logical succession
through the narrative, and it welds tales which may hith-
erto have been wholly unrelated (e.g. *Tiresias*, *Narcissus*
and *Echo*, or *Pentheus* and *Acoetes' Tale*) into a seemingly
unified and organic complex. So Ovid in a sense achieves
the effect of ἕν ἄεισμα διηνεκές without infringing Callimachus' veto, a novel achievement that fully justifies
the claim advanced in his prologue. The *Metamorphoses*
is a new and hybrid alternative, even rival, to epic.
Like certain African insects which congregate to produce
the perfect illusion of a flower, so the poem mimics the
forbidden fruit of epic, but adheres to Callimachean prin-
ciples at the same time. Instead of the steady progress
in time of an epic poem from A to B, e.g. from the Fall
of Troy to the Trojans' gaining a foothold in Italy,
seven years (Virgil, *Aeneid* 1.1 - 7), Ovid substitutes
what Coleman calls 'a general chronological drift',
launching the reader with maximum momentum into the body
of the poem by means of the introductory Creation-Flood-
Rebirth sequence, hypnotising him into imagining that
he is moving forward through the middle reaches of it,
and then imparting proper motion to him again once the
Trojan and post-Trojan (Roman) historical chapters begin
(11.192 ff.). The illusion of progress is there throughout.

In the matter of links between stories - 'a large
part of Ovid's game' as Wilkinson puts it (*Ovid Recalled*,
p. 149) and vital for sustaining continuity - the poet
shows himself astonishingly inventive. The epic parallel-
narrative device of a dum-clause or an interea is seldom
used (e.g. 3.316), though Ovid may occasionally want it
just for its epic colour (e.g. 8.547). The transitions
in Book 3 receive comment in the Notes. However, one
common type that is not represented in the book is the
mentioning of some object, either present or absent, by
the narrator or by some character in the story. For example, in Book 1 the tale of Daphne and the origin of

the laurel (an aetiological myth) is hung on the remark
that Apollo used to adorn his locks with any old tree,
since 'nondum laurus erat' (1.450); and in the same book
the tale of Syrinx and the origin of the pan-pipe (also
aetiological) arises out of Argus' interest in the instrument that Mercury is playing (1.686 f.). Besides
narrative links, however, thematic connexions are prominent in the poem. Family relationships may be included
here, but of greater importance are similarities in kind
(including the presence of the same character) between
stories which may be juxtaposed or on the contrary widely
separated, the thematic link then acting as a means of
bonding the blocks together.

Thus in Book 3 the person of Bacchus connects *Semele*, across the intervening *Tiresias* and *Narcissus and
Echo*, with *Pentheus* and *Acoetes' Tale*; the thematic link
is doubly strong here, as Bacchus is in fact one of Cadmus' family, Pentheus' cousin. In the complicated web
of stories told by Orpheus in Book 10, narrative links
are insignificant (they can afford to be, since it is
a song recital), but the whole is held together by the
theme of love - good and bad - and the presence of Venus
in many of the stories. The connexion with Orpheus' own
emotional situation completes the bonding within the
group, which forms a self-contained unit (10.1 - 11.66)
having only tenuous narrative links with what precedes
and follows.

The world Ovid creates in the *Metamorphoses* would
be a far less rich and fascinating one if he had stuck
rigidly to his declared intention of retailing stories
of transformations only. Although these account for the
vast majority, there are many which contain no transformation, while in a fair proportion the transformation is
a mere afterthought and cannot have been the criterion
for selection. For instance in Book 3 *Pentheus* has no
transformation at all: he is simply torn to pieces, without the compensating dignity of becoming, say, a flower
like Narcissus or Hyacinthus (10.209 ff.). Indeed, after
Book 1, Ovid quietly substitutes the notion of a mythological compendium or universal guidebook for that of a
specialised monograph. Of the several large-scale epic
'panels' in the poem, such as the second part of *Perseus*
(5.1 - 249), *The Calydonian Boar Hunt* (8.270 - 525),
Achilles and Cygnus (12.63 - 145) or *The Battle of Lap-
iths and Centaurs* (12.210 - 535), none seem to have been
chosen for a transformation, except possibly the first,
in which Perseus brings the fight to a close by turning
Phineus and his men to stone by means of the Gorgon's
head. Ovid's reasons for including such 'heroic' stories
are perhaps two: they were generally popular and demanded

a place in a mythological poem, despite its supposedly restricted programme; and they brought a highly desirable stiffening and solidity to a work which might otherwise collapse in a welter of heterogeneous episodes. These chunks of red-blooded Homeric action provide a form of articulation for the epic-sized body of the *Metamorphoses* quite separate from its narrative and chronological framework. Equally importantly, they afford a change of texture for the reader.

The variety of texture or tone is indeed one of the most striking features of the poem. Just as structurally the main need is to find some means of creating cohesion and the semblance of organic unity, so there is an opposite requirement in so long a poem - to secure as much tone- and colour-variation as possible. To restrict discussion to Book 3 alone, we have first the heroic story of Cadmus and the battle with the serpent, told in a slightly heightened epic style, with copious echoes of Virgil and a borrowing from Apollonius Rhodius. The transition to *Actaeon* is (for once) made conspicuous by a variety of rhetorical devices and a solemn, moralising *sententia* (135 - 7), all of which prepares us for a change, not so much of style as of approach. *Actaeon* is still 'heroic' (including ecphrasis, hunting scene, catalogue), but, instead of the hard, virile, objective quality of *Cadmus*, the mood is now softer, gentler, more subjective and sympathetic: from a Homeric epic manner Ovid has switched to a Hellenistic, 'psychological' one. His interest is less in the physical aspect of the transformation *per se* than in how it affects and expresses the victim's mental condition. This preoccupation with the psychology of the sufferer is characteristic of Alexandrian writing. *Semele* on the other hand is nothing but a black Divine Comedy, featuring a philandering and fatuously magnanimous Jupiter and his scheming and malignant shrew of a wife, and a silly, vain, greedy mortal; the nurse-figure, Beroë, is an inspired importation from tragedy quite as much as from epic, though her pedigree is impeccably Virgilian. The story of Narcissus brings the book to a long, dreamy standstill while we listen to the mental gyrations of this anti-heroic figure. Here is the apotheosis of the interior monologue, developed from Euripides but owing much also to the *suasoria*, or mock-deliberative speech pondering the best course of action (a favourite school exercise of Ovid's, Seneca tells us). Much of the writing is rhetorical, wit mixing with pathos, neatly turned paradox expressing simplicity of mind. We are invited to feel pity for Narcissus - but still more to applaud the writer's adroitness in creating a character at once foolish and pathetic. With *Pentheus* we enter the world of tragedy, though a less sadly tragic world than

that of Euripides' *Bacchae*, for the character of Pentheus
is drawn far less sympathetically by Ovid. The issues
are more black and white here: the bullying blasphemer
gets his just deserts. This does not, however, lessen
the impact of some powerful writing in the final scene
where the sense of fright and madness comes through all
the effects of Grand Guignol. The book ends with a quiet
'moral', a small moment of respite after the bloody horror
of Pentheus' death. *Acoetes' Tale* is straight objective
narration, in the manner of a Homeric Hymn, its violence
no more disturbing that that of the epic scenes.

Ovid's purpose, then, is to entertain, to delight,
to help us escape from our everyday world into one of
the imagination, which is nevertheless *geographically*
the world with which the ancient reader was familiar.
The poem is shot through with humour of every kind, from
sophisticated verbal wit to the situations of farce. The
gods come in for consistently disrespectful handling,
whether as comedians or as villains (e.g. Diana in the
present book). Unlike the gods of Virgil, they do not
constitute a 'divine machinery', controlling but remote
from events on earth; on the contrary, they are inextric-
ably involved in affairs, initiating action and precipit-
ating crisis by their own desires, jealousies, pride,
and other failings. Transformation might even be described as a curse visited on mortals by the immortals,
but that would suggest that Ovid had a theological motive
for choosing the subject, which is untrue. The ancient
world - a very beautiful world of woods and water - into
which Ovid transports us is ancient only in its atmosphere
and 'props'. Ovid's mind, unlike that of Virgil or Livy,
does not become antique when writing about antiquity; he
remains outside and apart from the past which he yet loves
and understands so well. Indeed the characters of the
Metamorphoses (as is more apparent in other books, for
Book 3 is slightly exceptional) are largely 'modern' men
and women, with the attitudes and beliefs prevailing in
Augustan Rome. The tension between setting and personality
is one of the most piquant aspects of the poem, and one
which helps to prevent it becoming stale. The background
may come round again and again, but the actors are end-
lessly varied, three-dimensional, interesting, and extraordinarily like ourselves.

3. *THE POETRY.*

With the exception of the primitive Saturnian measure, all the metres of Latin poetry (being borrowed from
the Greeks) are quantitative, i.e. they are made up of
various patterns (feet) of long (-) and short (ᵛ) syllables. The dactylic hexameter consists of six feet,
each of which must be either a *dactyl* (-ᵛᵛ) or a *spondee*
(--). The line's normal scheme is:-

1	2	3	4	5	6
-ᵛᵛ	-ᵛᵛ	-ᵛᵛ	-ᵛᵛ	-ᵛᵛ	-ᵛ
- -	- -	- -	- -		

The sixth foot is nominally a spondee, but the very last
syllable is *anceps* ('unfixed') and may in practice be
short, giving an actual *trochee* (-ᵛ). If the fifth foot
dactyl is replaced by a spondee, which occurs only rarely,
the hexameter is described as 'spondaic' (e.g. 3.184 or
669).

Every verse must have a *caesura*, i.e. a break between
words not coinciding with a division between feet, in the
third or fourth foot. There are normally secondary caesurae elsewhere in the verse, though hardly ever in the
fifth and sixth feet, but without a caesura in either the
third or fourth foot, the line disintegrates. The commonest caesura in Ovid's and in all Latin hexameters is after
the first syllable of the third foot; this is called a
'strong' or 2½ caesura, e.g.:-

īamquĕ dĕ̄us pŏsĭ̄|tā ¦ fāl|lācĭs ĭmagĭnĕ|taurī   1

hāc dŭcĕ|cārpĕ vĭ̄as ¦ ēt|quā rĕquĭ̄ēvĕrĭt|hērbā   12

The other places where the main caesura occurs are after
the second syllable of the third foot, called a 'weak'
or 'trochaic' or 2¾ caesura, and after the first syllable
of the fourth foot, called a 'late' or 3½ caesura. It is
not possible in fact to illustrate from Book 3 a line
which does not exhibit both these caesurae together. Ovid
always 'protects' the weak with a following 3½ caesura,
e.g.:-

prōcŭbŭĭt tĕnĕrāquĕ ¦ lătūs ¦ sūm|ĭsĭt ĭn|hērbā   24

īnfāus|tō tĕtĭgĕrĕ ¦ grădū ¦ dĕ̄m|issăque ĭn|ūndās   36

One might choose to scan the former verse with the main
caesura at 2¾ and the latter with the main caesura at 3½
in conformity with the phrasing, but strictly the caesura
has nothing to do with sense or sense-pauses but is a

purely metrical (or mechanical) phenomenon. The following examples from the *Aeneid* show independent 2¼ and 3½
caesurae respectively:-

ăccĭpĭēs sēcūră ǀ vŏcābĭtŭr|hīc quŏquĕ|vōtĭs   1.290

ĭntĕrdūm gĕnŭa|ĭmpĕdĭŭnt ǀ cūr|sūmquĕ rĕcūsānt   12.747

Scansion depends on knowing the length of the syllables in a line. The rules for determining whether a
syllable is to be marked long or short ('heavy' or 'light')
are as follows:

A. *Within words*:

1. If the syllable contains a long vowel or a diphthong,
it is long.

2. If the syllable contains a short vowel, it is short,
unless rules (3) or (4) apply.

3. If the vowel is followed by two consonants or a
double consonant (X, Z), the syllable is long, unless
rule (4) applies.

4. If a short vowel is followed by the combinations cl,
fl, pl, br, cr, dr, fr, gr, pr, tr, the syllable can be
either short or long as required; e.g. patrēs, which can
be divided either as pāt-res, when rule (3) applies, or
as pă-tres, with tr counting (like the other combinations
listed) as a quasi-single consonant. This rule is invalid
for prepositional prefixes which end in a consonant, since
such prefixes count as separate words (see B.2 below).

B. *At the ends of words*:

1. If the word ends with a consonant other than m and
the next word begins with a vowel or a diphthong, the
quantity of the last syllable is determined by rules (1)
and (2) above.

2. If the word ends with a consonant (including m) and
the next word begins with a consonant, the last syllable
is long.

3. If the word ends in a short open vowel and the next
word begins with one of the combinations listed in (4)
above or with bl, the last syllable stays short (there
are a few - a very few - exceptions to this rule).

4. If the word ends in a vowel or in -am, -em, -im (rare)
or -um and the next word begins with a vowel or diphthong,

the last syllable is *elided*, i.e. disappears for purposes
of scansion (and pronunciation). (Elision may occur across
the caesura, e.g. 109, mōx ŭmĕrī pĕc̣tūsque ¦ ŏnẹ̆rātăquĕ¦
brācchĭă̦|tēlīs.) Occasionally elision does not take place
and there is *hiatus* instead (e.g. 184). Where the next
word is es or est, we speak of *prodelision*, not elision,
since it was not the final vowel or -am (etc.) that dis-
appeared in pronunciation, but the vowel of es or est,
e.g. 225 mŏră̆ est (= mŏrāst), 253 ambĭgŭo est (= āmbĭgŭōst)
or 291, dĕŏrŭm est (= dĕŏrūmst). (Some editors prefer to
print the 'condensed' spelling.)

Ovid's hexameters show extremely few metrical irreg-
ularities (none that are not deliberate and artistic)
and they are on the whole easier to scan than almost any
other poet's. One reason for this is that he makes very
sparing use of elision (less than half the amount used by
Virgil). Final short syllables are the most frequently
elided, and he is fond of prodelision; final syllables in
-am (etc.) are seldom elided, and final syllables ending
in a long vowel hardly at all (in marked contrast to Virgil).

The rhythm of Ovid's verses is noticeably more dactylic than Virgil's. If we represent a dactyl by D and
a spondee by S, we find that the two poets' eight favourite
metrical *schemata* or patterns for the first four feet of
the line are significantly different:-

	Ovid		Virgil	
1	DDSS	(13.1%)	DSSS	(14.4%)
2	DSSS		DDSS	
3	DSSD		DSDS	
4	DSDS		SDSS	
5	DDSD		SSSS	
6	DDDS		DDDS	
7	DSDD		SSDS	
8	DDDD	(5.7%)	SDDS	(5.8%)

Ovid has a dactylic first foot in each of his top eight
schemata, Virgil in only four of his; Ovid a dactylic
fourth foot in four, Virgil in none. There are 20 dactyls
to 12 spondees in Ovid's list, 20 spondees to 12 dactyls
in Virgil's. Ovid plainly seeks dactyls in preference to
spondees, speed and lightness in preference to weight and
statuesqueness (just as he seeks smoothness rather than
ruggedness by reducing elisions to a minimum). His hexameters have been called the hexameters of an elegist,
with some justification; but in fact he succeeds in catching, to a degree quite unmatched by other Latin poets,
the rapidity, suppleness and grace of Homer's hexameters,
in which again dactyls greatly prevail over spondees (22
to 10 in the eight commonest *schemata*). The un-Roman

quality of Ovid's verse, far from being inconsistent with
his subject-matter (as has been claimed), on the contrary
complements it: for Greek myths, 'Greek' hexameters.
Thus Ovid observes (as he can, for he has the technical
expertise) an aspect of the fundamental literary law of
decorum ('appropriateness') that his predecessors had
perhaps either been unaware of or regarded as a needless
and anyway unattainable refinement.

4. *NOTE ON THE TEXT*.

The text of the *Metamorphoses* has suffered little
in transmission. It descends ultimately from at least
two slightly differing versions of the poem, both authen-
tic but between which Ovid did not have time to make a
final choice. The effects of this 'double recension',
however, are not apparent in Book 3, except possibly at
143 ff. (see Notes). Our Mss. - 390 have been catalogued -
are conventionally divided into two classes, O and X.
The former contain the prose summaries (*narrationes*,
argumenta) or their titles of a certain Lactantius; these
go back to the fifth or sixth century and seem to have
formed part of a definitive edition-with-commentary which
rejected the alternative verses that are preserved in
the other branch of the tradition. The text of the O
family is generally superior to that of the very much
larger and amorphous X group, but the latter offers a
substantial number of preferable readings. The oldest
witnesses are the Berne fragment of c. 850 - 870 A.D.,
which contains the first 56 lines of Book 3, the Paris
fragment of the 9th or early 10th century with 1.81 -
193 and 2.67 - 160, and the Leipzig fragment (dated to
the 10th century by the majority of experts), which carries only 3.131 - 52.

The text printed here is a new one, the result not
of any original labours with the manuscripts but simply
of an examination of Hugo Magnus' edition of 1914 and
D. A. Slater's *Towards a Text of the Metamorphosis* [sic]
of Ovid (1927). Other texts, e.g. that prepared by G. M.
Edwards for J. P. Postgate's *Corpus Poetarum Latinorum*,
tom. 1 (1894), have also been referred to. Asterisks
in the left-hand margin beside a verse indicate the ex-
istence of a textual problem. There are four in all.
(1) The order of words given in 66 follows the example
of 672 and so avoids the impossible *homoeoteleuton* (repeated ending) lentae spinae in the middle of the line,
which was allowed by Edwards. (2) In 99 metu has been

put for diu, which yields poor sense, whereas metu pavidus is both apt and paralleled elsewhere. (3) The majority reading at 688 - 9, pavidum gelidumque trementi/
corpore vixque meum, offends against classical practice
by assigning two similar epithets to the same object (me
understood) and seems to violate grammar by giving the
abl. corpore an adj. in the acc. The solution offered
preserves everything except the terminations of the words,
which are the most likely parts to have suffered corruption through abbreviation. (4) The biggest crux comes at
641 - 2, where the uncorrected tradition has quis te furor
inquit Acoete/pro se quisque timet. The first part of
this, 'quis te furor' inquit, 'Acoete', is unexceptionable,
but we require a speaker's name, a verb for furor, and
something to attach pro se quisque timet meaningfully to
what goes before. The change of timet to tenet gives
sense of a sort, but the passage remains unsatisfactory.
Among emendations proposed is 'quis te furor' inquit Oph-
eltes/'persequiturve timor?', but any solution which has
to exclude Acoete must be suspect. Slater's remedy (op.
cit., p. 43), to transpose 641 and 642, creates new dif-
ficulties.

    Other textual points mentioned in the Notes of this
edition will be found enclosed in square brackets. With
regard to orthography, consonantal u is written as v
(the name spelt Agave in English has been retained as
Agauë, as the au represents a Greek diphthong); prepositional prefixes are usually assimilated (e.g. as-sumo
for ad-sumo, sum-mitto for sub-mitto); and where the evidence is trustworthy for the spelling of the acc. pl. of
3rd declension words in -īs (as opposed to -ēs), this has
been adopted; Ovid's own practice, like (allegedly) Virgil's, may have varied.

5. *GENEALOGICAL TABLES.*

A. *The House of Cadmus*

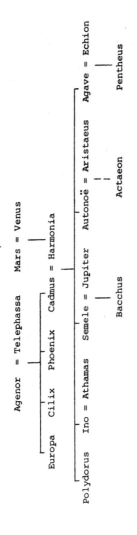

```
                    Agenor = Telephassa      Mars = Venus
                              |                    |
          ┌──────┬───────┬────┴────┐         Cadmus = Harmonia
       Europa  Cilix  Phoenix                       |
                              ┌──────────┬──────────┬──────────┐
                         Ino = Athamas  Semele = Jupiter  Autonoë = Aristaeus  Agave = Echion
        Polydorus                              |                |                      |
                                            Bacchus          Actaeon              Pentheus
```

B. *The Spartids*

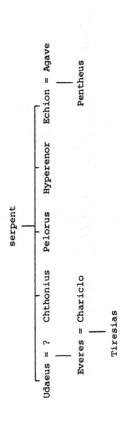

```
                                        serpent
                    ┌──────────┬──────────┬──────────┬──────────┐
               Udaeus = ?  Chthonius  Pelorus  Hyperenor  Echion = Agave
                    |                                             |
           Everes = Chariclo                                  Pentheus
                    |
                Tiresias
```

6. SELECT BIBLIOGRAPHY

Bömer, F.:   *P. Ovidi Nasonis Metamorphosen, Buch I - III*,
                      Heidelberg, 1969.

Coleman, R. G. G.:   Structure and Intention in the *Metamorphoses*,
                      Classical Quarterly 21 (1971) 461 - 477.

Galinsky, G. K: *Ovid's Metamorphoses, an Introduction to the
                      Basic Aspects*, Oxford, 1976.

Higham, T. F.:   Ovid and Rhetoric, in *Ovidiana, Recherches sur
                      Ovide*, ed. N. I. Herescu, Paris, 1958, 32 - 48.

Hollis, A. S.:   *Ovid Metamorphoses Book VIII*, Oxford, 1970.

Kenney, E. J.:   The Style of the *Metamorphoses*, in *Ovid*, ed.
                      J. W. Binns, London, 1973, 116 - 153.

Otis, Brooks: *Ovid as an Epic Poet*, Cambridge, 1970[2].

Rose, H. J.:   *A Handbook of Greek Mythology, including its
                      Extension to Rome*, London, 1958[6].

Thibault, J. C.:   *The Mystery of Ovid's Exile*, Berkeley, Cali-
                      fornia, 1964.

Wilkinson, L. P.:   *Ovid Recalled* (especially ch. 7), Cambridge,
                      1955 (abridged under the title *Ovid Surveyed*).

Wilkinson, L. P.:   The World of the *Metamorphoses*, in *Ovidiana,
                      Recherches sur Ovide*, ed. N. I. Herescu, Paris,
                      1958, 231 - 244.

On the question of elision of final syllables, see in particular
W. S. Allen, *Vox Latina*, Cambridge, 1965, 30-31 and 78ff.

M E T A M O R P H O S E S   Book III

Cadmus

Iamque deus posita fallacis imagine tauri
se confessus erat Dictaeaque rura tenebat,
cum pater ignarus Cadmo perquirere raptam
imperat et poenam, si non invenerit, addit
5 exilium, facto pius et sceleratus eodem.
   orbe pererrato - quis enim deprendere possit
furta Iovis? - profugus patriamque iramque parentis
vitat Agenorides Phoebique oracula supplex
consulit et quae sit tellus habitanda requirit.
10 'bos tibi' Phoebus ait 'solis occurret in arvis,
nullum passa iugum curvique immunis aratri.
hac duce carpe vias et, qua requieverit herba,
moenia fac condas Boeotiaque illa vocato.'
vix bene Castalio Cadmus descenderat antro;
15 incustoditam lente videt ire iuvencam
nullum servitii signum cervice gerentem.
subsequitur pressoque legit vestigia gressu
auctoremque viae Phoebum taciturnus adorat.
iam vada Cephisi Panopesque evaserat arva;
20 bos stetit et tollens speciosam cornibus altis
ad caelum frontem mugitibus impulit auras,
atque ita respiciens comites sua terga sequentis
procubuit teneraque latus summisit in herba.
Cadmus agit grates peregrinaeque oscula terrae
25 figit et ignotos montes agrosque salutat.
sacra Iovi facturus erat; iubet ire ministros
et petere e vivis libandas fontibus undas.
   silva vetus stabat nulla violata securi
et specus in medio virgis ac vimine densus,
30 efficiens humilem lapidum compagibus arcum,

uberibus fecundus aquis, ubi conditus antro
Martius anguis erat, cristis praesignis et auro.
igne micant oculi, corpus tumet omne venenis,
tres vibrant linguae, triplici stant ordine dentes.
35 quem postquam Tyria lucum de gente profecti
infausto tetigere gradu demissaque in undas
urna dedit sonitum, longo caput extulit antro
caeruleus serpens horrendaque sibila misit.
effluxere urnae manibus, sanguisque relinquit
40 corpus et attonitos subitus tremor occupat artus.
ille volubilibus squamosos nexibus orbes
torquet et immensos saltu sinuatur in arcus,
ac media plus parte levis erectus in auras
despicit omne nemus tantoque est corpore, quanto,
45 si totum spectes, geminas qui separat Arctos.
nec mora; Phoenicas, sive illi tela parabant
sive fugam, sive ipse timor prohibebat utrumque,
occupat. hos morsu, longis complexibus illos,
hos necat afflatu funesti tabe veneni.
50   fecerat exiguas iam sol altissimus umbras.
quae mora sit sociis miratur Agenore natus
vestigatque viros. tegimen derepta leoni
pellis erat, telum splendenti lancea ferro
et iaculum teloque animus praestantior omni.
55 ut nemus intravit letataque corpora vidit
victoremque supra spatiosi corporis hostem
tristia sanguinea lambentem vulnera lingua,
'aut ultor vestrae, fidissima corpora, mortis,
aut comes' inquit 'ero.' dixit, dextraque molarem
60 sustulit et magnum magno conamine misit.
illius impulsu cum turribus ardua celsis
moenia mota forent; serpens sine vulnere mansit,
loricaeque modo squamis defensus et atrae
duritia pellis validos cute reppulit ictus.
65 at non duritia iaculum quoque vicit eadem,

*quod medio fixum spinae curvamine lentae
constitit, et totum descendit in ilia ferrum.
ille dolore ferox caput in sua terga retorsit
vulneraque aspexit fixumque hastile momordit,
70 idque ubi vi multa partem labefecit in omnem,
vix tergo eripuit; ferrum tamen ossibus haesit.
    tum vero, postquam solitas accessit ad iras
causa recens, plenis tumuerunt guttura venis
spumaque pestiferos circumfluit albida rictus,
75 terraque rasa sonat squamis, quique halitus exit
ore niger Stygio vitiatas inficit auras.
ipse modo immensum spiris facientibus orbem
cingitur, interdum longa trabe rectior astat,
impete nunc vasto ceu concitus imbribus amnis
80 fertur et obstantis proturbat pectore silvas.
cedit Agenorides paulum spolioque leonis
sustinet incursus instantiaque ora retardat
cuspide praetenta; furit ille et inania duro
vulnera dat ferro figitque in acumine dentes.
85 iamque venenifero sanguis manare palato
coeperat et virides aspergine tinxerat herbas;
sed leve vulnus erat, quia se retrahebat ab ictu
laesaque colla dabat retro plagamque sedere
cedendo arcebat nec longius ire sinebat,
90 donec Agenorides coniectum in gutture ferrum
usque sequens pressit, dum retro quercus eunti
obstitit et fixa est pariter cum robore cervix.
pondere serpentis curvata est arbor et imae
parte flagellari gemuit sua robora caudae.

The Spartoi

95   dum spatium victor victi considerat hostis,
vox subito audita est (neque erat cognoscere promptum

unde, sed audita est): 'quid, Agenore nate, peremptum
serpentem spectas? et tu spectabere serpens.'
*ille metu pavidus pariter cum mente colorem
100 perdiderat gelidoque comae terrore rigebant;
ecce viri fautrix superas delapsa per auras
Pallas adest motaeque iubet supponere terrae
vipereos dentes, populi incrementa futuri.
paret et, ut presso sulcum patefecit aratro,
105 spargit humi iussos, mortalia semina, dentes.
inde - fide maius - glaebae coepere moveri,
primaque de sulcis acies apparuit hastae.
tegmina mox capitum picto nutantia cono,
mox umeri pectusque onerataque bracchia telis
110 existunt, crescitque seges clipeata virorum.
sic, ubi tolluntur festis aulaea theatris,
surgere signa solent primumque ostendere vultus,
cetera paulatim, placidoque educta tenore
tota patent imoque pedes in margine ponunt.
115 territus hoste novo Cadmus capere arma parabat;
'ne cape' de populo, quem terra creaverat, unus
exclamat 'nec te civilibus insere bellis.'
atque ita terrigenis rigido de fratribus unum
comminus ense ferit; iaculo cadit eminus ipse.
120 hunc quoque qui leto dederat, non longius illo
vivit et expirat modo quas acceperat auras;
exemploque pari furit omnis turba, suoque
Marte cadunt subiti per mutua vulnera fratres.
iamque brevis vitae spatium sortita iuventus
125 sanguineam tepido plangebant pectore matrem,
quinque superstitibus, quorum fuit unus Echion.
is sua iecit humo monitu Tritonidis arma
fraternaeque fidem pacis petiitque deditque.
hos operis comites habuit Sidonius hospes,
130 cum posuit iussam Phoebeis sortibus urbem.

Actaeon

iam stabant Thebae; poteras iam, Cadme, videri
exilio felix. soceri tibi Marsque Venusque
contigerant; huc adde genus de coniuge tanta,
tot natas natosque et, pignora cara, nepotes,
135 hos quoque iam iuvenes. sed scilicet ultima semper
expectanda dies homini est dicique beatus
ante obitum nemo supremaque funera debet.
prima nepos inter tot res tibi, Cadme, secundas
causa fuit luctus alienaque cornua fronti
140 addita, vosque canes satiatae sanguine erili.
at bene si quaeras, Fortunae crimen in illo,
non scelus, invenies; quod enim scelus error habebat?
mons erat infectus variarum caede ferarum,
iamque dies medius rerum contraxerat umbras
145 et sol ex aequo meta distabat utraque,
cum iuvenis placido per devia lustra vagantis
participes operum compellat Hyantius ore:
'lina madent, comites, ferrumque cruore ferarum,
fortunamque dies habuit satis. altera lucem
150 cum croceis invecta rotis Aurora reducet,
propositum repetemus opus; nunc Phoebus utraque
distat idem meta finditque vaporibus arva.
sistite opus praesens nodosaque tollite lina.'
iussa viri faciunt intermittuntque laborem.
155 vallis erat piceis et acuta densa cupressu,
nomine Gargaphie, succinctae sacra Dianae,
cuius in extremo est antrum nemorale recessu,
arte laboratum nulla; simulaverat artem
ingenio natura suo, nam pumice vivo
160 et levibus tofis nativum duxerat arcum.
fons sonat a dextra, tenui perlucidus unda,
margine gramineo patulos incinctus hiatus.
hic dea silvarum venatu fessa solebat

virgineos artus liquido perfundere rore.
165 quo postquam subiit, nympharum tradidit uni
armigerae iaculum pharetramque arcusque retentos;
altera depositae subiecit bracchia pallae,
vincla duae pedibus demunt; nam doctior illis
Ismenis Crocale sparsos per colla capillos
170 colligit in nodum, quamvis erat ipsa solutis.
excipiunt laticem Nepheleque Hyaleque Ranisque
et Psecas et Phiale funduntque capacibus urnis.
dumque ibi perluitur solita Titania lympha,
ecce nepos Cadmi dilata parte laborum
175 per nemus ignotum non certis passibus errans
pervenit in lucum; sic illum fata ferebant.
qui simul intravit rorantia fontibus antra,
sicut erant nudae, viso sua pectora nymphae
percussere viro subitisque ululatibus omne
180 implevere nemus circumfusaeque Dianam
corporibus texere suis; tamen altior illis
ipsa dea est colloque tenus supereminet omnis.
qui color infectis adversi solis ab ictu
nubibus esse solet aut purpureae aurorae,
185 is fuit in vultu visae sine veste Dianae.
quae, quamquam comitum turba stipata suarum,
in latus obliquum tamen astitit oraque retro
flexit et, ut vellet promptas habuisse sagittas,
quas habuit, sic hausit aquas vultumque virilem
190 perfudit spargensque comas ultricibus undis
addidit haec cladis praenuntia verba futurae:
'nunc tibi me posito visam velamine narres,
si poteris narrare, licet.' nec plura minata
dat sparso capiti vivacia cornua cervi,
195 dat spatium collo summasque cacuminat aures,
cum pedibusque manus, cum longis bracchia mutat
cruribus et velat maculoso vellere corpus.
additus et pavor est. fugit Autonoeius heros

et se tam celerem cursu miratur in ipso.
200 ut vero vultus et cornua vidit in unda,
'me miserum' dicturus erat; vox nulla secuta est.
ingemuit; vox illa fuit, lacrimaeque per ora
non sua fluxerunt. mens tantum pristina mansit.
quid faciat? repetatne domum et regalia tecta,
205 an lateat silvis? pudor hoc, timor impedit illud.
    dum dubitat, videre canes; primique Melampus
Ichnobatesque sagax latratu signa dedere,
Cnosius Ichnobates, Spartana gente Melampus.
inde ruunt alii rapida velocius aura,
210 Pamphagos et Dorceus et Oribasos, Arcades omnes,
Nebrophonosque valens et trux cum Laelape Theron
et pedibus Pterelas et naribus utilis Agre
Hylaeusque ferox nuper percussus ab apro
deque lupo concepta Nape pecudesque secuta
215 Poemenis et natis comitata Harpyia duobus
et substricta gerens Sicyonius ilia Ladon
et Dromas et Canache Sticteque et Tigris et Alce
et niveis Leucon et villis Asbolos atris
praevalidusque Lacon et cursu fortis Aello
220 et Thoos et Cyprio velox cum fratre Lycisce
et nigram medio frontem distinctus ab albo
Harpalos et Melaneus hirsutaque corpore Lachne
et patre Dictaeo sed matre Laconide nati
Labros et Argiodus et acutae vocis Hylactor,
225 quosque referre mora est. ea turba cupidine praedae
per rupes scopulosque adituque carentia saxa,
quaque est difficilis, quaque est via nulla, sequuntur.
ille fugit; per quae fuerat loca nota secutus,
heu, famulos fugit ipse suos. clamare libebat
230 'Actaeon ego sum, dominum cognoscite vestrum.'
verba animo desunt; resonat latratibus aether.
prima Melanchaetes in tergo vulnera fecit,
proxima Therodamas; Oresitrophos haesit in armo

(tardius exierant, sed per compendia montis
235 anticipata via est). dominum retinentibus illis
cetera turba coit confertque in corpore dentes.
iam loca vulneribus desunt; gemit ille sonumque,
(etsi non hominis, quem non tamen edere possit
cervus,) habet maestisque replet iuga nota querelis
240 et genibus pronis supplex similisque roganti
circumfert tacitos tamquam sua bracchia vultus.
at comites rapidum solitis hortatibus agmen
ignari instigant oculisque Actaeona quaerunt
et velut absentem certatim Actaeona clamant
245 (ad nomen caput ille refert) et abesse queruntur
nec capere oblatae segnem spectacula praedae.
vellet abesse quidem, sed adest; velletque videre,
non etiam sentire canum fera facta suorum.
undique circumstant mersisque in corpore rostris
250 dilacerant falsi dominum sub imagine cervi,
nec nisi finita per plurima vulnera vita
ira pharetratae fertur satiata Dianae.

Semele

rumor in ambiguo est. aliis violentior aequo
visa dea est, alii laudant dignamque severa
255 virginitate vocant; pars invenit utraque causas.
sola Iovis coniunx non tam culpetne probetne
eloquitur, quam clade domus ab Agenore ductae
gaudet et a Tyria collectum paelice transfert
in generis socios odium. subit ecce priori
260 causa recens, gravidamque dolet de semine magni
esse Iovis Semelen. dum linguam ad iurgia solvit,
'profeci quid enim totiens per iurgia?' dixit.
'ipsa petenda mihi est; ipsam, si maxima Iuno
rite vocor, perdam, si me gemmantia dextra

265 sceptra tenere decet, si sum regina Iovisque
et soror et coniunx - certe soror. at, puto, furto est
contenta, et thalami brevis est iniuria nostri.
concipit; id deerat; manifestaque crimina pleno
fert utero et mater, quod vix mihi contigit, uno
270 de Iove vult fieri. tanta est fiducia formae.
fallat eam faxo, nec sum Saturnia, si non
ab Iove mersa suo Stygias penetrabit in undas.'
    surgit ab his solio fulvaque recondita nube
limen adit Semeles; nec nubes ante removit
275 quam simulavit anum posuitque ad tempora canos
sulcavitque cutem rugis et curva trementi
membra tulit passu. vocem quoque fecit anilem
ipsaque erat Beroe, Semeles Epidauria nutrix.
ergo ubi captato sermone diuque loquendo
280 ad nomen venere Iovis, suspirat et 'opto,
Iuppiter ut sit' ait, 'metuo tamen omnia; multi
nomine divorum thalamos iniere pudicos.
nec tamen esse Iovem satis est; det pignus amoris,
si modo verus is est, quantusque et qualis ab alta
285 Iunone excipitur, tantus talisque rogato
det tibi complexus suaque ante insignia sumat.'
talibus ignaram Iuno Cadmeida dictis
formarat; rogat illa Iovem sine nomine munus.
cui deus 'elige' ait; 'nullam patiere repulsam,
290 quoque magis credas, Stygii quoque conscia sunto
numina torrentis. timor et deus ille deorum est.'
laeta malo nimiumque potens perituraque amantis
obsequio Semele 'qualem Saturnia' dixit
'te solet amplecti, Veneris cum foedus initis,
295 da mihi te talem.' voluit deus ora loquentis
opprimere; exierat iam vox properata sub auras.
ingemuit; neque enim non haec optasse neque ille
non iurasse potest. ergo maestissimus altum
aethera conscendit vultuque sequentia traxit

300 nubila, quis nimbos immixtaque fulgora ventis
addidit et tonitrus et inevitabile fulmen.
qua tamen usque potest, vires sibi demere temptat
nec, quo centimanum deiecerat igne Typhoea,
nunc armatur eo; nimium feritatis in illo est.
305 est aliud levius fulmen, cui dextra Cyclopum
saevitiae flammaeque minus, minus addidit irae;
tela secunda vocant superi. capit illa domumque
intrat Agenoream. corpus mortale tumultus
non tulit aetherios donisque iugalibus arsit.
310 imperfectus adhuc infans genetricis ab alvo
eripitur, patrioque tener - si credere dignum est -
insuitur femori maternaque tempora complet.
furtim illum primis Ino matertera cunis
educat; inde datum nymphae Nyseides antris
315 occuluere suis lactisque alimenta dedere.

Tiresias

dumque ea per terras fatali lege geruntur
tutaque bis geniti sunt incunabula Bacchi,
forte Iovem memorant diffusum nectare curas
seposuisse gravis vacuaque agitasse remissos
320 cum Iunone iocos et 'maior vestra profecto est
quam quae contingit maribus' dixisse 'voluptas.'
illa negat. placuit quae sit sententia docti
quaerere Tiresiae; venus huic erat utraque nota.
nam duo magnorum viridi coeuntia silva
325 corpora serpentum baculi violaverat ictu,
deque viro factus - mirabile - femina septem
egerat autumnos. octavo rursus eosdem
vidit et 'est vestrae si tanta potentia plagae'
dixit, 'ut auctoris sortem in contraria mutet,
330 nunc quoque vos feriam.' percussis anguibus isdem

forma prior rediit genetivaque venit imago.
arbiter hic igitur sumptus de lite iocosa
dicta Iovis firmat. gravius Saturnia iusto
nec pro materia fertur doluisse, suique
335 iudicis aeterna damnavit lumina nocte.
at pater omnipotens (neque enim licet irrita cuiquam
facta dei fecisse deo) pro lumine adempto
scire futura dedit poenamque levavit honore.

Narcissus and Echo

ille per Aonias fama celeberrimus urbes
340 irreprehensa dabat populo responsa petenti.
prima fide vocisque ratae temptamina sumpsit
caerula Liriope, quam quondam flumine curvo
implicuit clausaeque suis Cephisos in undis
vim tulit. enixa est utero pulcherrima pleno
345 infantem, nymphis iam tunc qui posset amari,
Narcissumque vocat. de quo consultus, an esset
tempora maturae visurus longa senectae,
fatidicus vates 'si se non noverit' inquit.
vana diu visa est vox auguris; exitus illam
350 resque probat letique genus novitasque furoris.
namque ter ad quinos unum Cephisius annum
addiderat poteratque puer iuvenisque videri.
multi illum iuvenes, multae cupiere puellae;
sed fuit in tenera tam dura superbia forma,
355 nulli illum iuvenes, nullae tetigere puellae.
aspicit hunc trepidos agitantem in retia cervos
vocalis nymphe, quae nec reticere loquenti
nec prius ipsa loqui didicit, resonabilis Echo.
corpus adhuc Echo, non vox, erat; et tamen usum
360 garrula non alium, quam nunc habet, oris habebat,
reddere de multis ut verba novissima posset.

fecerat hoc Iuno, quia, cum deprendere vellet
sub Iove saepe suo nymphas in monte iacentis,
illa deam longo prudens sermone tenebat,
365 dum fugerent nymphae. postquam hoc Saturnia sensit,
'huius' ait 'linguae, qua sum delusa, potestas
parva tibi dabitur vocisque brevissimus usus',
reque minas firmat. tamen haec in fine loquendi
ingeminat voces auditaque verba reportat.
370   ergo ubi Narcissum per devia rura vagantem
vidit et incaluit, sequitur vestigia furtim,
quoque magis sequitur, flamma propiore calescit,
non aliter quam cum summis circumlita taedis
admotas rapiunt vivacia sulphura flammas.
375 o quotiens voluit blandis accedere dictis
et mollis adhibere preces. natura repugnat
nec sinit incipiat; sed, quod sinit, illa parata est
expectare sonos, ad quos sua verba remittat.
forte puer comitum seductus ab agmine fido
380 dixerat 'ecquis adest?' et 'adest' responderat Echo.
hic stupet, utque aciem partes dimittit in omnes,
voce 'veni' magna clamat; vocat illa vocantem.
respicit et rursus nullo veniente 'quid' inquit
'me fugis?' et totidem, quot dixit, verba recepit.
385 perstat et alternae deceptus imagine vocis
'huc coeamus' ait, nullique libentius umquam
responsura sono 'coeamus' rettulit Echo,
et verbis favet ipsa suis egressaque silva
ibat, ut iniceret sperato bracchia collo.
390 ille fugit fugiensque 'manus complexibus aufer;
ante' ait 'emoriar, quam sit tibi copia nostri.'
rettulit illa nihil nisi 'sit tibi copia nostri.'
spreta latet silvis pudibundaque frondibus ora
protegit et solis ex illo vivit in antris;
395 .sed tamen haeret amor crescitque dolore repulsae,
et tenuant vigiles corpus miserabile curae,

adducitque cutem macies et in aera sucus
corporis omnis abit. vox tantum atque ossa supersunt.
vox manet; ossa ferunt lapidis traxisse figuram.
400 inde latet silvis nulloque in monte videtur.
omnibus auditur; sonus est, qui vivit in illa.
    sic hanc, sic alias undis aut montibus ortas
luserat hic nymphas, sic coetus ante viriles.
inde manus aliquis despectus ad aethera tollens
405 'sic amet ipse licet, sic non potiatur amato'
dixerat. assensit precibus Rhamnusia iustis.
fons erat illimis, nitidis argenteus undis,
quem neque pastores neque pastae monte capellae
· contigerant aliudve pecus, quem nulla volucris
410 nec fera turbarat nec lapsus ab arbore ramus.
gramen erat circa, quod proximus umor alebat,
silvaque sole locum passura tepescere nullo.
hic puer, et studio venandi lassus et aestu,
procubuit faciemque loci fontemque secutus.
415 dumque sitim sedare cupit, sitis altera crevit,
dumque bibit, visae correptus imagine formae
spem sine corpore amat; corpus putat esse, quod unda est.
astupet ipse sibi vultuque immotus eodem
haeret, ut e Pario formatum marmore signum.
420 spectat humi positus geminum, sua lumina, sidus
et dignos Baccho, dignos et Apolline crines
impubesque genas et eburnea colla decusque
oris et in niveo mixtum candore ruborem,
cunctaque miratur quibus est mirabilis ipse.
425 se cupit imprudens et, qui probat, ipse probatur,
dumque petit, petitur pariterque accendit et ardet.
irrita fallaci quotiens dedit oscula fonti;
in mediis quotiens visum captantia collum
bracchia mersit aquis nec se deprendit in illis.
430 quid videat, nescit; sed quod videt, uritur illo,
atque oculos idem, qui decipit, incitat error.

credule, quid frustra simulacra fugacia captas?
quod petis, est nusquam; quod amas, avertere, perdes.
ista repercussae, quam cernis, imaginis umbra est.
435 nil habet ista sui; tecum venitque manetque,
tecum discedet, si tu discedere possis.
non illum Cereris, non illum cura quietis
abstrahere inde potest, sed opaca fusus in herba
spectat inexpleto mendacem lumine formam,
440 perque oculos perit ipse suos paulumque levatus
ad circumstantes tendens sua bracchia silvas
'ecquis, io silvae, crudelius' inquit 'amavit?
scitis enim et multis latebra opportuna fuistis.
ecquem, cum vestrae tot agantur saecula vitae,
445 qui sic tabuerit, longo meministis in aevo?
et placet et video, sed quod videoque placetque
non tamen invenio; tantus tenet error amantem.
quoque magis doleam, nec nos mare separat ingens
nec via nec montes nec clausis moenia portis.
450 exigua prohibemur aqua. cupit ipse teneri;
nam quotiens liquidis porreximus oscula lymphis,
hic totiens ad me resupino nititur ore.
posse putes tangi; minimum est, quod amantibus obstat.
quisquis es, huc exi. quid me, puer unice, fallis,
455 quove petitus abis? certe nec forma nec aetas
est mea quam fugias, et amarunt me quoque nymphae.
spem mihi nescioquam vultu promittis amico,
cumque ego porrexi tibi bracchia, porrigis ultro.
cum risi, arrides; lacrimas quoque saepe notavi
460 me lacrimante tuas, nutu quoque signa remittis,
et quantum motu formosi suspicor oris,
verba refers aures non pervenientia nostras.
iste ego sum; sensi, nec me mea fallit imago.
uror amore mei, flammas moveoque feroque.
465 quid faciam? roger, anne rogem? quid deinde rogabo?
quod cupio, mecum est; inopem me copia fecit.

o utinam a nostro secedere corpore possem.
votum in amante novum: vellem, quod amamus, abesset.
iamque dolor vires adimit, nec tempora vitae
470 longa meae superant primoque extinguor in aevo.
nec mihi mors gravis est posituro morte dolores;
hic, qui diligitur, vellem diuturnior esset.
nunc duo concordes anima moriemur in una.'
dixit et ad faciem rediit male sanus eandem
475 et lacrimis turbavit aquas, obscuraque moto
reddita forma lacu est; quam cum vidisset abire,
'quo refugis? remane, nec me, crudelis, amantem
desere' clamavit; 'liceat, quod tangere non est,
aspicere et misero praebere alimenta furori.'
480 dumque dolet, summa vestem deduxit ab ora
nudaque marmoreis percussit pectora palmis.
pectora traxerunt roseum percussa ruborem,
non aliter quam poma solent, quae candida parte,
parte rubent, aut ut variis solet uva racemis
485 ducere purpureum nondum matura colorem.
quae simul aspexit liquefacta rursus in unda,
non tulit ulterius, sed ut intabescere flavae
igne levi cerae matutinaeque pruinae
sole tepente solent, sic attenuatus amore
490 liquitur et tecto paulatim carpitur igni;
et neque iam color est mixto candore rubori
nec vigor et vires et quae modo visa placebant,
nec corpus remanet, quondam quod amaverat Echo.
quae tamen ut vidit, quamvis irata memorque,
495 indoluit, quotiensque puer miserabilis 'eheu'
dixerat, haec resonis iterabat vocibus 'eheu';
cumque suos manibus percusserat ille lacertos,
haec quoque reddebat sonitum plangoris eundem.
ultima vox solitam fuit haec spectantis in undam:
500 'heu frustra dilecte puer' totidemque remisit
verba locus, dictoque 'vale' 'vale' inquit et Echo.

ille caput viridi fessum summisit in herba;
lumina mors clausit domini mirantia formam.
tum quoque se, postquam est inferna sede receptus,
505 in Stygia spectabat aqua. planxere sorores
Naides et sectos fratri posuere capillos,
planxerunt Dryades; plangentibus assonat Echo.
iamque rogum quassasque faces feretrumque parabant;
nusquam corpus erat. croceum pro corpore florem
510 inveniunt foliis medium cingentibus albis.

Pentheus

cognita res meritam vati per Achaidas urbes
attulerat famam nomenque erat auguris ingens.
spernit Echionides tamen hunc ex omnibus unus,
contemptor superum Pentheus, praesagaque ridet
515 verba senis tenebrasque et cladem lucis ademptae
obicit. ille movens albentia tempora canis
'quam felix esses, si tu quoque luminis huius
orbus' ait 'fieres, ne Bacchica sacra videres.
namque dies aderit, quam non procul auguror esse,
520 qua novus huc veniat, proles Semeleia, Liber;
quem nisi templorum fueris dignatus honore,
mille lacer spargere locis et sanguine silvas
foedabis matremque tuam matrisque sorores.
eveniet; neque enim dignabere numen honore,
525 meque sub his tenebris nimium vidisse quereris.'
talia dicentem proturbat Echione natus.
dicta fides sequitur responsaque vatis aguntur.
Liber adest festisque fremunt ululatibus agri;
turba ruit mixtaeque viris matresque nurusque
530 vulgusque proceresque ignota ad sacra feruntur.
'quis furor, anguigenae, proles Mavortia, vestras
attonuit mentes?' Pentheus ait; 'aerane tantum

aere repulsa valent et adunco tibia cornu
et magicae fraudes, ut, quos non bellicus ensis,
535 non tuba terruerit, non strictis agmina telis,
femineae voces et mota insania vino
obscenique greges et inania tympana vincant?
vosne, senes, mirer, qui longa per aequora vecti
hac Tyron, hac profugos posuistis sede penates,
540 nunc sinitis sine Marte capi? vosne, acrior aetas,
o iuvenes, propiorque meae, quos arma tenere,
non thyrsos, galeaque tegi, non fronde, decebat?
este, precor, memores qua sitis stirpe creati,
illiusque animos, qui multos perdidit unus,
545 sumite serpentis. pro fontibus ille lacuque
interiit; at vos pro fama vincite vestra.
ille dedit leto fortes, vos pellite molles
et patrium retinete decus. si fata vetabant
stare diu Thebas, utinam tormenta virique
550 moenia diruerent ferrumque ignisque sonarent.
essemus miseri sine crimine, sorsque querenda,
non celanda, foret lacrimaeque pudore carerent.
at nunc a puero Thebae capientur inermi,
quem neque bella iuvant nec tela nec usus equorum,
555 sed madidus murra crinis mollesque coronae
purpuraque et pictis intextum vestibus aurum.
quem quidem ego actutum - modo vos absistite - cogam
assumptumque patrem commentaque sacra fateri.
an satis Acrisio est animi contemnere vanum
560 numen et Argolicas venienti claudere portas,
Penthea terrebit cum totis advena Thebis?
ite citi' (famulis hoc imperat), 'ite ducemque
attrahite huc vinctum. iussis mora segnis abesto.'
        hunc avus, hunc Athamas, hunc cetera turba suorum
565 corripiunt dictis frustraque inhibere laborant.
acrior admonitu est irritaturque retenta
et crescit rabies moderaminaque ipsa nocebant.

sic ego torrentem, qua nil obstabat eunti,
lenius et modico strepitu decurrere vidi;
570 at quacumque trabes obstructaque saxa tenebant,
spumeus et fervens et ab obice saevior ibat.
ecce cruentati redeunt et, Bacchus ubi esset,
quaerenti domino Bacchum vidisse negarunt.
'hunc' dixere 'tamen comitem famulumque sacrorum
575 cepimus' et tradunt manibus post terga ligatis
sacra dei quendam Tyrrhena gente secutum.
aspicit hunc Pentheus oculis quos ira tremendos
fecerat, et quamquam poenae vix tempora differt,
'o periture tuaque aliis documenta dature
580 morte' ait, 'ede tuum nomen nomenque parentum
et patriam morisque novi cur sacra frequentes.'

Acoetes' tale: Bacchus and the sailors

ille metu vacuus 'nomen mihi' dixit 'Acoetes,
patria Maeonia est, humili de plebe parentes.
non mihi quae duri colerent pater arva iuvenci,
585 lanigerosve greges, non ulla armenta reliquit.
pauper et ipse fuit linoque solebat et hamis
decipere et calamo salientis ducere pisces.
ars illi sua census erat. cum traderet artem,
"accipe quas habeo, studii successor et heres,"
590 dixit "opes", moriensque mihi nihil ille reliquit
praeter aquas; unum hoc possum appellare paternum.
mox ego, ne scopulis haererem semper in isdem,
addidici regimen dextra moderante carinae
flectere, et Oleniae sidus pluviale Capellae
595 Taygetenque Hyadasque oculis Arctonque notavi
ventorumque domos et portus puppibus aptos.
forte petens Delon Chiae telluris ad oras
applicor et dextris adducor litora remis

doque levis saltus udaeque immittor harenae.
600 nox ibi consumpta est. Aurora rubescere primo
coeperat; exsurgo laticesque inferre recentis
admoneo monstroque viam quae ducat ad undas.
ipse, quid aura mihi tumulo promittat ab alto
prospicio comitesque voco repetoque carinam.
605 "adsumus en" inquit sociorum primus Opheltes,
utque putat, praedam deserto nactus in agro
virginea puerum ducit per litora forma.
ille mero somnoque gravis titubare videtur
vixque sequi. specto cultum faciemque gradumque;
610 nil ibi, quod credi posset mortale, videbam.
et sensi et dixi sociis: "quod numen in isto
corpore sit, dubito; sed corpore numen in isto est.
quisquis es, o faveas nostrisque laboribus adsis.
his quoque des veniam." "pro nobis mitte precari"
615 Dictys ait, quo non alius conscendere summas
ocior antemnas prensoque rudente relabi.
hoc Libys, hoc flavus, prorae tutela, Melanthus,
hoc probat Alcimedon et, qui requiemque modumque
voce dabat remis, animorum hortator, Epopeus,
620 hoc omnes alii; praedae tam caeca cupido est.
"non tamen hanc sacro violari pondere pinum
perpetiar" dixi; "pars hic mihi maxima iuris",
inque aditu obsisto. furit audacissimus omni
de numero Lycabas, qui Tusca pulsus ab urbe
625 exilium dira poenam pro caede luebat.
is mihi, dum resto, iuvenali guttura pugno
rupit et excussum misisset in aequora, si non
haesissem, quamvis amens, in fune retentus.
impia turba probat factum. tum denique Bacchus
630 (Bacchus enim fuerat), veluti clamore solutus
sit sopor aque mero redeant in pectora sensus,
"quid facitis? quis clamor?" ait; "qua, dicite, nautae,
huc ope perveni? quo me deferre paratis?"

"pone metum" Proreus "et quos contingere portus
635 ede velis" dixit; "terra sistere petita."
"Naxon" ait Liber "cursus advertite vestros.
illa mihi domus est, vobis erit hospita tellus."
per mare fallaces perque omnia numina iurant
sic fore, meque iubent pictae dare vela carinae.
640   dextra Naxos erat; dextra mihi lintea danti
"quid facis, o demens? quis te furor" inquit, "Acoete,"
*pro se quisque "tenet? laevam pete." maxima nutu
pars mihi significat, pars quid velit aure susurrat.
obstipui "capiat"que "aliquis moderamina" dixi,
645 meque ministerio scelerisque artisque removi.
increpor a cunctis totumque immurmurat agmen;
e quibus Aethalion "te scilicet omnis in uno
nostra salus posita est" ait et subit ipse meumque
explet opus Naxoque petit diversa relicta.
650 tum deus illudens, tamquam modo denique fraudem
senserit, e puppi pontum prospectat adunca
et flenti similis "non haec mihi litora, nautae,
promisistis" ait, "non haec mihi terra rogata est.
quo merui poenam facto? quae gloria vestra est,
655 si puerum iuvenes, si multi fallitis unum?"
iamdudum flebam; lacrimas manus impia nostras
ridet et impellit properantibus aequora remis.
per tibi nunc ipsum (nec enim praesentior illo
est deus) adiuro, tam me tibi vera referre
660 quam veri maiora fide. stetit aequore puppis
haud aliter quam si siccum navale teneret.
illi admirantes remorum in verbere perstant
velaque deducunt geminaque ope currere temptant.
impediunt hederae remos nexuque recurvo
665 serpunt et gravidis distingunt vela corymbis.
ipse racemiferis frontem circumdatus uvis
pampineis agitat velatam frondibus hastam.
quem circa tigres simulacraque inania lyncum

pictarumque iacent fera corpora pantherarum.
670 exiluere viri, sive hoc insania fecit
sive timor, primusque Medon nigrescere coepit
corpore et expresso spinae curvamine flecti.
incipit huic Lycabas: "in quae miracula" dixit
"verteris?" et lati rictus et panda loquenti
675 naris erat, squamamque cutis durata trahebat.
at Libys obstantis dum vult obvertere remos,
in spatium resilire manus breve vidit et illas
iam non esse manus, iam pinnas posse vocari.
alter ad intortos cupiens dare bracchia funes
680 bracchia non habuit truncoque repandus in undas
corpore desiluit; falcata novissima cauda est,
qualia dimidiae sinuantur cornua lunae.
undique dant saltus multaque aspergine rorant
emerguntque iterum redeuntque sub aequora rursus
685 inque chori ludunt speciem lascivaque iactant
corpora et acceptum patulis mare naribus efflant.
de modo viginti (tot enim ratis illa ferebat)
restabam solus. *pavidum gelidoque trementem
corpore vixque meo firmat deus "excute" dicens
690 "corde metum Diamque tene." delatus in illam
accessi sacris Baccheaque sacra frequento.'

Pentheus (concluded)

'praebuimus longis' Pentheus 'ambagibus aures'
inquit, 'ut ira mora vires absumere posset.
praecipitem, famuli, rapite hunc cruciataque diris
695 corpora tormentis Stygiae demittite nocti.'
protinus abstractus solidis Tyrrhenus Acoetes
clauditur in tectis; et dum crudelia iussae
instrumenta necis ferrumque ignesque parantur,
sponte sua patuisse fores lapsasque lacertis

700 sponte sua fama est nullo solvente catenas.
perstat Echionides nec iam iubet ire, sed ipse
vadit, ubi electus facienda ad sacra Cithaeron
cantibus et clara bacchantum voce sonabat.
ut fremit acer equus, cum bellicus aere canoro
705 signa dedit tubicen, pugnaeque assumit amorem,
Penthea sic ictus longis ululatibus aether
movit, et audito clamore recanduit ira.
    monte fere medio est, cingentibus ultima silvis,
purus ab arboribus, spectabilis undique campus.
710 hic oculis illum cernentem sacra profanis
prima videt, prima est insano concita cursu,
prima suum misso violavit Penthea thyrso
mater et 'o geminae' clamavit 'adeste sorores.
ille aper, in nostris errat qui maximus agris,
715 ille mihi feriendus aper.' ruit omnis in unum
turba furens; cunctae coeunt trepidumque sequuntur,
iam trepidum, iam verba minus violenta loquentem,
iam se damnantem, iam se peccasse fatentem.
saucius ille tamen 'fer opem, matertera' dixit,
720 'Autonoe; moveant animos Actaeonis umbrae.'
illa quis Actaeon nescit dextramque precantis
abstulit; Inoo lacerata est altera raptu.
non habet infelix quae matri bracchia tendat,
trunca sed ostendens deiectis vulnera membris
725 'aspice, mater' ait. visis ululavit Agaue
collaque iactavit movitque per aera crinem
avulsumque caput digitis complexa cruentis
clamat 'io comites, opus hoc victoria nostra est.'
non citius frondes autumni frigore tactas
730 iamque male haerentes alta rapit arbore ventus,
quam sunt membra viri manibus direpta nefandis.
    talibus exemplis monitae nova sacra frequentant
turaque dant sanctasque colunt Ismenides aras.

ABBREVIATIONS (Notes and Vocabulary)

abl.,	ablative	*intrans.,*	intransitive
acc.,	accusative	*lit.,*	literal(ly)
act.,	active	*m.,*	masculine
adj.,	adjective, -al	*Ms, Mss.,*	manuscript(s)
adv.,	adverb, -ial	*n.,*	neuter
conj.,	conjunction	*neg.,*	negative
dat.,	dative	*nom.,*	nominative
dep.,	deponent	*part.,*	participle, -ial
dir.,	direct	*pass.,*	passive
f.,	feminine	*perf.,*	perfect
fut.,	future	*pers.,*	person
gen.,	genitive	*pluperf.,*	pluperfect
imper.,	imperative	*pl.,*	plural
imperf.,	imperfect	*prep.,*	preposition, -al
impers.,	impersonal	*pres.,*	present
indecl.,	indeclinable	*pron.,*	pronoun
indic.,	indicative	*s.,*	singular
indir.,	indirect	*subj.,*	subjunctive
infin.,	infinitive	*subst.,*	substantive (adj. or part.
interrog.,	interrogative		as noun)
		trans.,	transitive

Names and works of ancient authors are printed in full with the exceptions
of Virgil (*.Ecl.* = *Eclogues, Georg.* = *Georgics, Aen.* = *Aeneid*) and Ovid
himself (*Am.* = *Amores, Ars Am.* = *Ars Amatoria, Rem. Am.* = *Remedia Amoris,
Her.* = *Heroides, Tr.* = *Tristia, Epp.* = *Epistulae ex Ponto, Fasti* in full);
references to Book III of the *Metamorphoses* are given as line numbers
only and to other books by number (e.g. 8.270) without naming the work.
Works listed in the bibliography are cited simply by author's surname
and date of publication. On points of syntax and grammar the following
abbreviations are used:

> GL = Gildersleeve and Lodge, *Latin Grammar* , 1948[3]
> K = Kennedy, *The Revised Latin Primer*, ed. Mountford, 1931
> W = Woodcock, *A New Latin Syntax*, 1959

NOTES

Cadmus, 1 - 95

The first sentence bridges the end of *The Rape of Europa* (2.836 ff.) and the beginning of *Cadmus*. We leave Europa shortly after her arrival in Crete; her subsequent marriage to Asterius, king of the island, does not concern the poet. Europa's father, Agenor of Tyre, is introduced solely to provide a causal link between tales. Whatever sources Ovid may have consulted for the legend of Cadmus, the essentials of his account can be found in Euripides, *Phoenissae* 638 ff. (second choral ode), a play which Accius had translated into Latin, and in Euripides' *Bacchae*.

1 - 3 *iamque* ... *cum*: a formula of transition in Virgil (e.g. *Aen.* 3.588, 5.327, 7.25), though not exclusively poetic. The *cum* is 'inverted', i.e. the *cum* clause is logically the principal one, though grammatically subordinate (GL 581, K 434 (c), W 237).

1 *deus*: Jupiter, to whom Europa presently bore three sons, Minos, Rhadamanthys and Sarpedon. * *posita fallacis imagine tauri*: cf. 250 (of Actaeon) *'falsi dominum sub imagine cervi'*. In both the adj. may be given to *imagine* in translation ('the fraudulent shape of ... '). *posita = deposita*, simple for compound verb; cf. 88, 333, 396 etc.

2 *Dictaea*: from *Dicte*, a mountain in eastern Crete, where the infant Jupiter was tended by nymphs in a cave and suckled by the goat Amalthea (a variant located the cave on Mt. Ida); see Callimachus, *Hymns* 1.46 ff., *Fasti* 5.111 ff., Apollodorus 1.1.6 f. Here the adj. simply means 'Cretan'. * *tenebat*: 'was residing, resting in'.

3 *perquirere*: an act. infin. (prolative) after *impero* is poetic syntax (GL 532 note 1); cf. 89 and 94; found once in Virgil: *Aen.* 7.35 f.

4 *poenam*: in apposition to *exilium*. * *si non invenerit*: perf. subj., the condition being in Virtual (Partial) Oratio Obliqua, primary (vivid) sequence (GL 663.2b); the apodosis can be supplied from *exilium*. *si non = nisi*, but with an added emphasis on the neg. ('if you don't find her ... '); often however *si non* is substituted for purely metrical reasons (cf. 271 or 627). (For the rules in prose, see GL 591, K 442.)

5 *facto eodem*: abl. of respect (GL 397, K 235, W 55). * *pius et sceleratus*: Agenor displays proper parental concern for Europa, but unnatural harshness towards

Cadmus. For a similar oxymoron cf. 8.477 '(*Thestias*)
impietate pia est' (by putting her brothers' lives above
that of her son Meleager).

6 *orbe pererrato*: humorous exaggeration at the expense of
epic's heroic conventions; cf. *Aen*. 2.295 (of Aeneas)
'(*moenia*) *magna pererrato statues quae denique ponto*.'
According to Apollodorus (3.1.1 and 3.4.1), probably
drawing on the early mythographers Pherecydes and Hel-
lanicus, Cadmus and his two brothers Cilix and Phoenix
each took a different part of the world to search. Cadmus settled in Thrace with his mother Telephassa; on her
death he went south to Delphi to resume enquiries about
his sister, but was told to forget her and found a city.

6 - 7 *quis enim ... Iovis?*: for the subj. in questions of
this type, see GL 259, W 176. *furtum* here means an
illicit love affair, though with a play on the literal
sense, since Europa was actually stolen away; cf. 1.606
(Jupiter again) '*deprensi totiens ... furta mariti*'
and *Aen*. 10.91 '*foedera solvere furto*' (alluding to
Paris' adultery with and abduction of Helen).

7 *patriamque iramque*: redoubled -*que* reproduces the Homeric
τε ... τε; it is not a native Latin idiom. First found
in Ennius, the father of Latin hexameter epic, it then
recurs in Virgil, Ovid (cf. 128, 132, 414, 618 etc.),
Lucan and Statius. The first -*que* must not be translated.

8 *Agenorides*: patronymics form an important part of the
traditional apparatus of the epic style. They are often
sonorous and dignified, and may have an emotive value
(cf. *Aeneas Anchisiades* - *Aen*. 8.521 - or *Laomedontiaden
Priamum* - *Aen*. 8.158). Ovid employs them, and derived
adjs., in profusion to enrich the texture and associat-
ions of the narrative; see Kenney (1973) 126 f.

9 *requirit*: for the simple *quaerit*, as frequently in Ovid.

11 *aratri*: partitive gen. after *immunis*, as after *plenus*,
expers, *particeps* and the like (GL 374, W 73.3). The
phrase *curvi immunis aratri* amounts to much the same
as *nullum passa iugum*, with a small shift of focus.
This technique of 'theme and variation' is a notable
feature of both Ovid's and Virgil's writing; see Kenney
(1973) 132 ff. For other examples in this book, see
17, 63 - 4, 83 - 4, 135 - 7, 226 - 7, 337 - 9, 464,
511 - 2, 662 - 3.

12 *carpe vias*: 'wend your way', another lofty Virgilian
phrase (e.g. *Aen*. 6.629), perhaps taken over from

Ennius. * *qua*: adv. (= *ubi*), not relative pron.
* *herba*: local abl. without prep. (GL 385 note 1, W
51.iv); contrast 23 '*latus summisit in herba*'.

13 *fac condas*: a familiar mode of command (GL 271.1, W 130),
foreign to true epic: 'see you found a city' (*moenia* =
urbem by metonymy). The fut. (or second) imper. *vocato*
is similarly, in this context, informal (GL 268.2).
The gods in the *Metamorphoses* converse easily with mortals, unless they have cause to be on their dignity.
* *Boeotia*: adj., here = 'Theban'. The name *Boeotia*
was anciently connected with βοῦς, 'ox'.

14 *vix bene*: *bene* may be ignored in translating. It intensifies or completes the sense of the verb ('fully descended',
i.e. 'finished descending'), the whole idea then being
modified by *vix*; cf. 2.47 '*vix bene desierat (loqui)*'.
After *vix* + pluperf. either *cum inversum* (see on 1 - 3
above) or a new sentence is the rule; the same applies
to *iam* + pluperf. (cf. 1 ff., 19 f., 85 ff.). * *Castalio antro*: the adj. *Castalius* is loosely used by the
Latin poets of the oracle of Apollo at Delphi, which
lay at some distance from the actual Castalian spring
or the rock-cut basin in which its waters were collected.
antrum denotes a cave or recess (cf. 31 and 37); Apollo
is supposed to have spoken from a chasm in early times
(cf. Livy 1.56.10 '*ex infimo specu vocem redditam ferunt*').
In the classical period the Holy-of-Holies (*adyton*, *pen-
etrale*) comprised a small chamber beneath a corner of
the temple at bedrock level in which his priestess (the
Pythia) sat on a tripod. For the abl. of separation or
place whence without prep., see GL 390, W 42.2.

15 *incūstōdītām*: an Ovidian coinage; other adjs. formed in
the same way (neg. *in* + past part.) include *irreprehensus*
(1.340), *inobservatus* (2.544) and *indevitatus* (2.605);
see Kenney (1973) 124 f. The slow, even, spondaic
rhythm of the epithet reinforces the image of the cow
ambling along (*lente ire*).

16 *servitii*: both Virgil (*Georg.* 3.168) and Tibullus (2.1.5)
have this metaphor of animals in bondage to mankind; it
goes back at least to the time of Aeschylus (*Prometheus*
463 f.).

17 *presso legit vestigia gressu*: a variation (with an added
detail) on *subsequitur*. *legit* = 'keeps to', 'follows'.
The abl. is one of manner; cf. 36 *infausto gradu* (GL
399, K 236, W 48). *presso* = 'checked', 'arrested', so
'slow'.

18 *adorat*: Cadmus addresses a (silent) prayer of thanks to

Apollo.

19 *Cephisi Panopesque*: Cephis(s)us was the name of several
   rivers in Greece; the Boeotian one rises on Mt. Oeta
   and flows south-east into Lake Copais (now drained).
   Panope or Panopeus was the old name of a town on the
   borders of Phocis, in which Delphi lay, and Boeotia;
   its later name was Phanoteus. For the gen. ending in
   -es, see GL 65, K 67. * *evaserat*: 'had passed', 'left
   behind'; the verb is more often intrans., + *ex*.

20 *stetit*: perf. of *sisto*, not *sto*; cf. *Aen*. 9.389 '(*Nisus*)
   ut stetit et frustra absentem respexit amicum,/"Euryale"
   (*inquit*)'. * *cornibus altis*: abl. of description or
   quality (GL 400, K 234, W 83).

22 *atque ita*: a connective formula much employed by Ovid,
   which has to be rendered according to context. Here =
   approximately *quo facto* (i.e. *fronte sublata mugituque
   edito*); cf. *Am*. 3.6.53 ('in this attitude') or *Rem. Am*.
   668 ('in her arms'); also 118 below (= *his dictis*).

23 *in herba*: although there is a strong sense of motion present, Ovid (as often) puts the abl. after *in*, not the
   acc.; cf. 90 '*coniectum in gutture ferrum*' or 236 '*confertque in corpore dentes*' (W 52.i).

24 *agit grates*: *grates agere* is correct for thanking a god,
   gratias agere for thanking a human. (The distinction
   is not always observed, and cannot be in dactylic verse,
   from which *grātiās* is excluded by its shape.)

25 *figit*: 'imprints'. * *ignotos*: the sense is that he is
   a stranger to the region, not that he has no idea where
   he is (cf. 24 *peregrinae terrae*).

26 *ministros*: the *comites* or *socii* (51) of Cadmus - introduced only to die and so motivate his combat with the
   dragon - are described as 'assistants' because they
   will participate in the sacrifice for which they seek
   water. They are not his servants or slaves, but of
   noble birth (cf. 538 f.).

27 *vivis*: 'fresh', 'running', as opposed to standing water.
   The adj. can also denote what is in its natural state,
   not worked or manufactured, e.g. *vivum saxum* (cf. 159).
   * *libandas*: water is required for ritual purposes when
   sacrificing the cow to Apollo. The gerundive retains
   much of its original sense of fitness, 'suitable-for-
   pouring', with which the notions of futurity and intention are closely bound up, 'that may/are to be poured'
   (W 203).

28 - 34 An ecphrasis or descriptive interlude, interrupting
the narrative, the equivalent of a scene-change in the
theatre. When the stage has been set, with the monster
peering out from his lair at the back, on come the actors (35). Such passages are a hallmark of epic, and
invariably begin with a formula of the type *est locus/
nemus/specus*, of which *silva ... stabat* is but a variant, and lead back into the main narrative through a
correlative adv. of place, e.g. *hic* or *illic* (here
quem ... lucum = huc). For other instances, see 155 -
65 *vallis erat ... quo*, 407 - 13 *fons erat ... hic*.
Besides epic (e.g. *Iliad* 2.811 ff., *Odyssey* 4.844 ff.,
Apollonius, *Argonautica* 1.936 ff., Ennius, *Annales* 24,
Aen. 1.530 ff. and 7.563 ff.), the ecphrasis features
in tragedy (e.g. Aeschylus, *Persae* 447 ff.), comedy
(e.g. Aristophanes, *Birds* 1473 ff.) and elegy (e.g.
Ars Am. 3.687 ff.).

28 *nulla violata securi*: the wood is a sacred grove; to fell
it would be sacrilege; cf. the story of Erysicthon (8.
739 ff.), who cut down an oak of Ceres and was punished
with insatiable hunger. For the abl. in -*i*, see GL 57.
2, K 44 note 1.

29 *in medio*: although *medium* does not appear to be used as
a subst. elsewhere by Ovid, this phrase is found in
Virgil (*Ecl.* 3.40, *Georg.* 3.16, *Aen.* 6.282), as is
medio + gen. (*Aen.* 3.354 *aulai medio* and 4.184 *caeli
medio*). *in medio* (*silvae*) is more likely to be right
than the easier variant *in media* (*silva*). * *virgis
ac vimine densus*: 'overgrown with branches and stems';
vimen = any pliant young woody shoot, e.g. of willow
or oak, from which baskets etc. can be woven. The
abl. with *densus* is instrumental, as with *plenus*, *cre-
ber* etc. (GL 401, W 43.1).

30 *efficiens ... arcum*: 'forming an arch with close-fitting
stones'. *compages* or *compago* is formed from *cum* and
the root *pag*, seen in *pango* (originally *pago*), *pegi*
(or *pepigi*), *pactum*, 'fasten'.

32 *Martius anguis*: the serpent or 'dragon' (not a fire-
breathing monster, as are the dragons in the myths of
many other countries) is the son of Ares (Mars); cf.
Euripides, *Phoenissae* 657, Apollodorus 3.4.1. The
origin of both the serpent's and Ares' connexion with
Thebes is obscure. It may go back to a phrase in
Homer, *Iliad* 4.407 τεῖχος ἄρειον. 'stronger' or 'Ares'
wall', which occurs in a reference to the attack on
Thebes by the Epigonoi or Sons of the Seven (Apollodorus 3.7.2 ff.). At any rate it gave the Theban
nobility a double claim to distinction - they were

both autochthonous (see the tale of the Spartoi, below)
and descendants of the God of War, patron of Homer's
Achaeans (the Mycenaean Greeks). * *cristis praesignis et auro*: hendiadys, 'wondrous with golden crest';
Euripides makes this crimson (*Phoenissae* 820 φοινικό-
λοφος). For the abl. of respect, cf. 5 above.

33 *venenis*: a 'distributive' pl. - every part of its body
contains a portion of the poison.

34 *tres vibrant linguae*: 'its three tongues (or 'three-
forked tongue') flicker in and out'. Such monsters
traditionally possess either three or a hundred heads,
tongues etc. The fashion starts with Homer, *Iliad* 11.
39 δράκων, κεφαλαὶ δέ οἱ ἦσαν/τρεῖς ἀμφιστρέφεες, ἑνὸς
αὐχένος ἐκπεφυυῖαι ('a serpent with three heads that
swivelled about, growing out of a single neck'), where
the poet is describing a shield-device.

This whole scene, down to 80, should be compared with
Virgil's picture of the twin snakes that destroy Lao-
coon and his sons (*Aen.* 2.204 ff.).

35 *Tyria de gente profecti*: lit. 'those who had departed
from the race of Tyre', so 'the Tyrian refugees'. The
part. is subst. (GL 437, W 101). With a phrase of
origin denoting a person or persons, like *de gente
Tyria*, *proficisci* would normally carry the figurative
sense of 'descend from' (e.g. *Aen.* 8.51 '*Arcades ...
genus a Pallante profectum*', i.e. *ortum* or *oriundum*).
Possibly this meaning is also present here, secondarily.

36 *infausto gradu*: the men's mission was an unpropitious
one. The epithet prepares the reader for the worst.

38 *caeruleus*: a dark greenish-blue, the colour too of Virgil's infernal *angues* (*Georg.* 4.482); it corresponds
roughly to the Greek κυάνεος, which is the hue of
Homer's beast (see on 34 above).

39 - 40 *effluxere, relinquit, occupat*: the perf. expresses
instantaneous action: the pitchers take no time at all
to fall. By contrast the onset of the physical and mental symptoms of terror occupies a measurable extent of
time. For this tense-pattern cf. *Aen.* 1.84 ff. '*incub-
uere mari totumque a sedibus imis/una Eurusque Notusque
ruunt creberque procellis/Africus, et vastos volvunt ad
litora fluctus*' and *Rem. Am.* 139 f. '*otia si tollas,
periere Cupidinis arcus,/contemptaeque iacent et sine
luce faces.*'

40 *attonitos*: the epithet is transferred from the men's
   minds to their limbs, a figure that results in consid-
   erable verbal economy and creates a sharp visual image
   of the physical attitudes of the group.

41 *ille*: marks change of subject, as commonly: 'The snake
   ... '; cf. 68, 83, 99, 228 etc. * *volubilibus nexi-*
   bus: 'in writhing arabesques', abl. of manner.
   * *orbes*: 'coils'.

42 *sinuatur*: 'curves itself' (= *se sinuat*). As Latin, unlike Greek, has no surviving middle voice, the passive
   is sometimes used to express the notion of doing something to or for oneself ('reflexive'). *erectus* in the
   next line is also middle, as are *cingitur* (78) and *fer-*
   tur (80) (GL 212 and 218, W 19.iii).

43 *media plus parte*: 'more than half its length', adv. *plus*
   with abl. of comparison (GL 398, K 231, W 78 and 79).

44 - 45 *tantoque ... Arctos*: i.e. *tantoque est corpore, quanto*
   est ille (si illum totum spectes), qui geminas Arctos
   separat. The abls. are descriptive (GL 400, K 234,
   W 83). Ovid aptly compares the serpent to the constellation Draco, which lies partly between the Great and
   Little Bears, Ursa Major and Minor (*Arcti*, f. pl., is
   their Greek name); cf. Cicero, *Aratea* fragment 8 '*has*
   inter, veluti rapido cum gurgite flumen,/torvu' Draco
   serpit subter superaque revolvens/sese conficiensque
   sinus e corpore flexos' (quoted in his own dialogue
   De Natura Deorum 2.106). Were this winding line of
   stars to be straightened out and seen at its full length
   (*si totum spectes*), that would give you the measure of
   the Theban monster - an amusingly grotesque fancy, characteristic of our author.

46 *nec mora*: an epic formula (also *haud mora, nulla mora*
   est) = *extemplo, protinus*. * *Phoenicăs*: Greek acc.
   pl. from nom. s. *Phoenix*.

46 - 47 *sive ... sive ... sive*: Ovid lists three reactions
   by the Tyrians, to which correspond the three means of
   death that follow in 48 - 9. For a similar, orderly
   three-fold structure see 77 - 9. However artificial,
   it helps to keep the narrative line from becoming entangled at moments of rapid and confused action.
   * *sive tela parabant, sive fugam*: a syllepsis ('zeugma')
   in which one verb governs two objects of different cat-
   egories (one concrete, one abstract). Ovid is fond of
   the figure; see Kenney (1973) 125. (Cf. 'He took his
   hat and his departure' - Dickens; 'Dost sometimes coun-
   sel take - and sometimes tea' - Pope.)

47 *utrumque*: n., referring to each of the two previous ideas,
   tela parare and *fugam parare*.

48 *occupat*: 'falls upon', with the accessory notion of striking first. Note the telling effect of holding over the
   verb (in shape a dactyl) so as to conclude the period
   at the end of the first foot.

49 *afflatu funesti tabe veneni*: *veneni* is gen. of quality
   (GL 365, K 249, W 84), dependent on *afflatu* (instrumental abl.). *tabe* is also abl. of instrument, governed
   by *funesti*. The involuted syntax should be dispensed
   with in translation: 'with its deadly, tainted, venom-
   laden breath'.

50 Time has passed: it is now noon. The line marks a new
   paragraph or change of scene, back to Cadmus.

51 *Agenore natus*: a periphrasis, identical in meaning with
   Agenorides (8); cf. *Echionides* 513 and *Echione natus*
   526 below. *satus*, *genitus*, *ortus* and *editus* are similarly
   constructed with an abl. of origin, e.g. 1.82 *satus
   Iapeto* (Prometheus), *Aen.* 9.639 *dis genitus* (Iulus);
   see GL 395, K 230, W 41.1.

52 *vestigat*: 'sets out after'.

52 - 53 *derepta leoni pellis*: cf. 81 *spolio leonis*. The dat.
   with such verbs of removing etc. is the indir. obj.
   (GL 345, W 61). *tegimen* stands in apposition to the
   phrase. With *erat* supply *ei* (dat. of possessor).

53 *telum*: in apposition to both *lancea* and *iaculum*.
   * *splendenti ferro*: descriptive abl.

54 *iaculum*: a throwing spear (*iacio*), as opposed to a thrust-
   ing spear.

55 *ut*: temporal; the clause has two parts, each with its
   verb, but the second is further subdivided, and the
   second member of this in turn expanded by the addition
   of a part. phrase (57). * *letata*: 'slain', a very
   rare verb, only found in Ovid and the pseudo-Virgilian
   Culex.

56 *supra*: adv. * *spatiosi corporis*: descriptive gen. The
   adj. often denotes size or bulk, not merely length or
   width; cf. 95 and *Rem. Am.* 421 '*parva necat morsu spat-
   iosum vipera taurum*'.

57 *tristia*: lit. 'saddening', so 'grievous', 'horrible'.

58 - 59 *aut* ... *aut*: Latin habitually puts alternative pro-
positions where English would turn one into a condition
('If I cannot avenge your deaths, in death I shall accompany you'); cf. 1.607 f. *'aut ego fallor/aut ego
laedor'*.

58 *fidissima corpora*: 'my most faithful stalwarts'. *corpus*
often connotes physical prowess or excellence; cf. *Aen.*
9.272 f. *'bis sex genitor lectissima matrum/corpora
captivosque dabit'*. We have now met *corpus* three times
in four lines, always in the fifth foot. A modern
writer would hardly let this stand, but the ancients
do not seem to have minded such casual repetitions (cf.
66 *fixum*, 69 *fixumque*; 92 *robore*, 94 *robora*; 372 *flamma*,
374 *flammas*; 681 *corpore*, 686 *corpora*, 695 *corpora*; or - one
of the most notorious instances - *Aen.* 1.103 - 16 *fluctus ... fluctu ... fluctus ... fluctibus ... fluctus*).

59 *molarem*: usually a millstone, but here just a large rock
(cf. *Aen.* 8.250 '*(Alcides) ramis vastisque molaribus
instat'*). The rock-throwing motif goes back to Homer,
who has Athene pick up a massive boundary stone and
fell Ares with it (*Iliad* 21.403 ff.). In his final combat with Aeneas, Turnus seizes the same but is unable
to propel it (*Aen.* 12.897 f. *'saxum antiquuum, ingens,
quod forte iacebat,/limes agro positus'*).

60 *magnus magno conamine misit*: 'with a mighty effort sent
the mighty object spinning'. Alliteration, assonance
(*a, o*) and rhythm all convey the impression of strain.
The ultimate model for the line, with its repetition
in different cases of *magnus*, is *Iliad* 16.776 (Cebrio-
nes) κεῖτο μέγας μεγαλωστί ('huge, and hugely spread,
he lay'). This Lucretius imitated at *De Rerum Natura*
1.741 *'et graviter magni magno cecidere ibi casu'*, followed by *Aen.* 5.447. Here, however, Ovid may have had
another, similar Lucretian verse in mind, *De Rerum Natura* 4.902 *'trudit agens magnam magno molimine navem'*.

62 *mota forent*: the pluperf. subj. expressing possibility
in the past (Past Potential) is very rare indeed in
classical Latin (GL 258 note 2, W 121 note ii). The sentence is equivalent to a concessive clause. *forem*
frequently replaces *essem* in compound tenses in potential, conditional or indirect constructions.

63 *modo*: abl. of *modus* + gen., 'in the manner of'; cf. Horace, *Odes* 4.2.27 f. *'ego apis Matinae/more modoque/...
carmina fingo'*.

64 *pellis ... cute*: virtual synonyms ('hide', 'skin'), a
pleonasm or *cumulatio*.

65 *duritia eadem*: instrumental abl. * *vicit*: 'stopped'.

66 *medio spinae curvamine lentae*: 'in the middle of his
   sinuously curving back' (cf. 672). *lentus* basically
   means 'yielding under pressure'. Hence, if the notion
   of reluctance to yield is uppermost, 'stiff', 'slow',
   'frigid', etc.; if that of giving way is stressed,
   'pliant', 'supple', 'wavy', etc.

67 *totum descendit*: 'went right down', 'buried itself com-
   pletely'. A Mycenaean (Bronze Age) hero like Cadmus
   has no business carrying any weapon of iron, but Ovid
   (like Virgil) is quite indifferent to such a trifling
   anachronism.

68 *dolore ferox*: 'frenzied with pain', causal abl. (GL 408,
   K 243, W 45).

69 *vulnera*: a poetic pl., adopted for the sake of the extra
   short syllables; for some judicious comments on such
   pls., see Kenney (1973) 128.

70 *partem in omnem*: adv., 'on all sides'.

71 *vix*: 'with difficulty' (= *aegre*). * *ossibus*: i.e. its
   rib-cage. The case may be either abl. or dat. (GL 346
   note 6).

72 ff. So far the serpent has been on the defensive; now it
   counter-attacks (*tum vero* introduces the 'second round'
   of the fight). Ovid builds up to a powerful climax
   which transcends his previous dramatic description of
   the Phoenicians' fate. Not only can he draw on a re-
   markably copious vocabulary but, like a good film di-
   rector, he also has a very exact, lucid and detailed
   mental picture of each successive phase of the struggle.
   Virgil's technique (*Aen.* 2.201 - 27) is different, for
   he concentrates rather on atmosphere and emotion. Ovid
   remains detached, Virgil is involved.

73 *causa recens*: sc. *irae*, 'this fresh source (of wrath)',
   i.e. the wound. The same phrase recurs at 260.

74 *rictus*: the pl. is explained by the fact that the mouth
   consists of two symmetrical jaws (GL 204 note 6).
   * *albidus*: a rare and prosaic synonym of *albus*, here
   only in Ovid. The verse forms a Golden Line (two nouns,
   each with an epithet, and a verb), of the AbVaB variety.
   Other Golden Lines are scattered throughout the book
   (e.g. 57, 125, 347, 439). Their role may be either emphatic (as here) or purely decorative.

75 *quique halitus*: for *halitusque qui*; in full: *halitus niger,
qui Stygio ore exit, auras vitiatas inficit.*

76 *inficit*: both 'stains' and 'infects'.   * *vitiatas*: proleptic or anticipatory, i.e. the logical syntax would
be *inficit et vitiat* or *infectas vitiat*. This is class-
ed as a hypallage by some ancient commentators, e.g.
Servius on *Georg.* 2.264 '*labefacta movens robustus iu-
gera fossor*' ('*hypallage: movens et labefaciens*').

77 - 79 *modo ... interdum ... nunc*: 'at one moment ... at another ... next'. More often, at least in prose, the
same word is repeated, e.g. Cicero, *Orator* 201 '*interdum enim cursus est in oratione incitatior, interdum
moderata ingressio.*'

77 *immensum spiris facientibus orbem*: instrumental abl. phrase
with *cingitur*, 'surrounds itself with its coils forming
a vast disc'. The beast lies coiled flat, its head and
neck at the centre.

78 *astat*: 'rears up'; cf. *Georg.* 3.545 '*attoniti squamis
astantibus hydri*' (= *horrentibus*, 'standing on end').

79 *impete*: an exclusively poetic form of the unmetrical
impetu (a gen. *impetis* also occurs).   * *ceu*: a simile-
word confined to serious poetry until Silver Latin.
* *concitus imbribus*: 'in spate'.

80 *proturbat*: 'thrusts aside', 'smashes through'; cf.
'*(Tiresian) proturbat Echione natus*' 526 below.

81 *spolio leonis*: see on 52 above. The gen. is objective
(GL 363.2, K 262, W 72.3).

82 *instantia ora*: a pl. of frequency: the serpent strikes
(*instare*) at Cadmus repeatedly.

83 *cuspide praetenta*: 'with outstretched lance' (he has used
his javelin), *cuspide* standing by synecdoche for the
whole weapon; cf. 1.227 '*obsidis unius iugulum mucrone
(= gladio) resolvit*'.

83 - 84 Theme and variation again: *vulnera dare ferro* = *dentes in acumine figere*. See on 11 above, and cf. 87 -
89 below. Note the triple alliteration of *f* (*littera
insuavissima*, as it was called) and *d*, the one mimick-
ing the noise emitted by the beast, the other emphasising the weapon's toughness (*duro*).

85 *venenifero palato*: abl. of separation.

87 - 92 The conclusion of the struggle is told in a single
long, complex sentence, the final stages being artic-
ulated by means of twin temporal clauses (*donec, dum*).
The first three lines illustrate the working of theme
and variation very well. The basic thought is 'the
wound was superficial, because the serpent took evas-
ive action', which is then repeated and elaborated.
Thus *colla dabat retro* = *se retrahebat*, the change from
the undifferentiated *se* to the specific *colla* giving a
sharper focus; *cedendo* reiterates this, while *plagam
sedere arcebat* picks up *leve vulnus erat*; finally *nec
longius ire sinebat* rephrases *plagam sedere arcebat*.

88 *sedere:* = *insidere*, 'penetrate', 'strike home', simple
for the compound verb. The construction of *arceo* +
prolative infin. is modelled on that of *prohibeo*.

89 *longius ire:* 'go, sink in further'.

91 *usque:* adv., correlative with *dum*, 'right on, until ... '
    * *retro eunti* = *cedenti* (subst., 'the retreating one',
    i.e. the serpent).

92 *pariter:* temporal.

93 - 94 *imae parte caudae:* 'with the extremity of its tail'.
    [*ima* (found in some Mss.) would normalise the grammar
    but leave *caudae* awkwardly stranded a long way from
    its governing abl.; *imae*, by its position, unites them.]

94 *flagellari sua robora:* 'that its trunk was being thrashed'.
An acc. and infin. construction after *gemo* is rare and
poetic; so too is a simple infin. *robora* is a poetic
pl., *metri gratia* (cf. 92 *robore*).

The Spartoi, 95 - 130

95 *dum considerat:* for the tense, see GL 570, K 430, W 221.

96 *vox:* in Euripides, *Bacchae* 1330a the prophecy is made by
Dionysus (Bacchus). Here the speaker seems to be the
spirit of the slain serpent, which has returned to the
earth that bore it. * *neque erat cognoscere promptum:*
the infin. is the subject; cf. *facile, leve* or *turpe
est* + infin. (GL 421 (c), K 366, W 25).

97 *unde:* shorthand for the clause *unde vox audita esset* (or
venisset, etc.), indir. question dependent on *cognoscere*.

98 *serpentem* ... *serpens*: the artistically varied repetition
of noun (change of case) and verb (change of voice and
tense) is designed to link the two sentences so as to
bring out the intimate connexion between present and
future events. The verse appropriately hisses and spits,
having six *s*'s, with secondary alliteration of the plos-
ive consonants *p* and *t*. A further subtlety is the chiasmus of the word order (ABba). The predicted metamorphosis of Cadmus (and his wife Harmonia) is recounted
in 4.563 ff., to conclude the Theban material in cyclic
fashion. Ovid incorrectly presents his transformation
as a punishment for killing Ares' beast; it was really
a form of deification or reward for a good and useful
life. See Apollodorus 3.5.4; Rose (1958) 185 f. * *et*:
for *etiam*.

99 *metu*: causal abl.

100 'My (his, their) blood ran cold' is a cliché of epic (e.g.
Aen. 10.452 and 12.905). Ovid, typically and deliberately, overdoes matters by depicting Cadmus as in addition white-faced, mentally incapacitated and with his
(long) hair on end. He has omitted three other traditional symptoms of fright, namely sweat (e.g. *Aen.* 3.
175, following Ennius, *Annales* 424), the shakes (e.g.
Aen. 3.29 f.) and loss of speech (e.g. *Aen.* 12.876).

101 *ecce*: 'suddenly', a common enough sense; cf. 174, 259,
10.210, *Am.* 1.5.9 (a parody of a divine epiphany like
Pallas' here), Horace, *Satires* 1.9.60, *Aen.* 2.203, 3.687,
8.81 (the Virgilian examples all with *autem*). * *viri*:
vir frequently does duty for the insignificant pronoun
is in epic verse; cf. 731 *membra viri* = *membra eius*.
* Pallas Athene (Minerva), the warrior goddess, is
the protectress of several heroes, most notably Ulysses.
Her association with Cadmus can be traced back to the
early lyric poet Stesichorus (*c.* 630 - *c.* 553 B.C.).
Note the scansion *Pallăs* (*-ădis*), as distinct from *Pal-
lās* (*-antis*), the son of Evander and victim of Turnus
(*Aen.* 8.104 ff., 10.442 ff.). * *motae*: the part. is
best rendered by another infin., 'to plough ... and'.
For the dat. (indir. obj.) expressing real motion with
a compound verb, see GL 347, K 220, W 62.

103 *populi incrementa futuri*: 'the seeds of a race-to-be'.
incrementum, from *in-cresco*, denotes either the result
of growth ('child', etc.) or the cause of it, as here
(cf. the variation at 105, *mortalia semina*).

104 *ut*: temporal (= *simul ac*).

105 *iussos dentes*: 'the teeth, as bidden'; cf. 1.399 '*et*

iussos lapides sua post vestigia mittunt.' The epithet
is transferred from subject ('he/they having been bidden') to object. [These examples guarantee the reading *iussam* at 130 (*iussus ... urbem* in some Mss.).]
For the appositional structure *iussos, mortalia semina,
dentes*, see on 420 below.

106 *fide maius*: lit. '(something that is) greater than belief', i.e. 'incredible though it be', neither an avowal
of disbelief nor an acknowledgement that a miracle oc-
curred, but simply 'a story teller's device for heigh-
tening the discourse', intellectually neutral like *mirabile dictu* or Virgil's '*si credere dignum est*' (*Aen.*
6.173), which is borrowed by Ovid at 311 below.

Ovid's description of the birth of the Spartoi or Sown
Men (cf. Pindar, *Hymns* Bergk fragment 30 σπαρτῶν ἱερὸν
γένος ἀνδρῶν - 'a holy race of sown men') owes much to
Apollonius' account of the ordeal of Jason in Colchis
(*Argonautica* 3.1334 ff., 1354 ff.). The teeth given to
him by King Aeetes (Medea's father) came from the self-
same serpent that Cadmus slew, Athene having divided
them between Cadmus and Aeetes (*Argonautica* 3.1176 - 90).

107 *prima*: virtually = *primum*, initiating a temporal series
continued by *mox ... mox* (= *deinde ... tum*). *primus*
often has the value of an adv.; cf. *Ars Am.* 2.467,
Rem. Am. 136, *Aen.* 4.169 and 5.42.

108 *picto nutantia cono*: strictly, neither *nutantia* nor *picto*
belongs with its noun; for the helmet does not wave
and its apex (*conus*, κῶνος) is not dyed. But perhaps
we should regard *conus* as standing for *crista* by metonymy. Homer had provided more than one description
of such a headpiece in the *Iliad* (e.g. 6.469 f. ταρ-
βήσας χαλκόν τε ἰδὲ λόφον ἱππιοχαίτην,/δεινὸν ἀπ᾽ ἀκρο-
τάτης κόρυθος νεύοντα νοήσας - 'fearful of the bronze
and the crest of horsehair, seeing it nodding terribly
from the top of the helmet').

110 *clipeata*: 'shield-bearing'. The *clipeus* was an early
Roman metal shield, circular in shape, and so not unlike certain Mycenaean shields; but the poets use the
term generically and unhistorically.

111 - 114 The simile follows what it illustrates; an equally
common pattern is for it to precede and to be hooked
up to the narrative by a correlative *sic, talis, haud
aliter*, etc. Ovid has chosen an anachronistic comparison, a favourite trick of his, and one of the ways in
which he prevents the reader from practising for long
that willing suspension of disbelief which most epic

poets are careful to foster; cf. his likening of Apollo
(1.533 ff.) to a greyhound, *canis Gallicus*, which (as
the epithet betrays) is out of place in mythological
Greece, or of Pyramus' gory suicide (4.121 ff.) to the
bursting of a lead water-main, an extraordinarily un-
(even anti-) epic picture. The simile at the corres-
ponding point in Apollonius' narrative (3.1359 - 62)
is by contrast perfectly conventional and 'proper' -
stars appearing in the sky after a snowstorm. Ovid's
is not whollyoriginal but owes much to *Georg.* 3.24 f.
'(*iuvat videre*) *scaena ut versis discedat frontibus
utque/purpurea intexti tollant aulaea Britanni*'.

111 *festis theatris*: 'in the theatre at holiday-time' (the
pl. expresses repetition, but is unnatural in English);
local abl. without *in*. The *ludi scaenici*, or public
festivals which included theatrical performances, were
the Megalensia (4th - 10th April), the Ludi Florales
(28th April - 3rd May), Apollinares (6th - 13th July),
Romani (4th - 19th September), and Plebei (4th - 17th
November). * *aulaea*: the curtain (or screen) in the
theatre of Ovid's day was lowered at the beginning of
a play (*aulaeum dimittere, premere*) and raised at its
end (*tollere, educere*).

112 *signa*: the figures embroidered on the curtain. We are
perhaps meant to hear the sound of the machinery used
to operate the curtain or the swish of the ascending
material in the succession of *s* sounds.

113 *cetera*: 'the rest of their bodies', i.e. shoulders, then
torso, then legs (not *cetera signa*). * *placido tenore*:
abl. of manner; such phrases are often best rendered
adverbially ('evenly and unhurriedly').

115 *hoste novo*: instrumental abl. (of persons: GL 214.2 and
401.1, W 44). *novus* here means both 'new', i.e. second
(Cadmus' first *hostis* was the serpent), and 'strange',
'startling' (cf. Cicero, *De Oratore* 1.137 '*nihil enim
dicam reconditum, ... nihil aut inauditum vobis aut cuiquam novum*').

116 *ne cape*: this form of prohibition is poetic and colloquial
(GL 270, K 350, W 128.ii); in prose normally *noli capere*.
* *de populo unus*: partitive, like *unus ex* (the use of
unus with partitive gen. is restricted: GL 372.2). The
repetition of the construction (with a change of case)
two lines later is deliberate, not careless (see on 58
above), for Ovid wishes to convey the idea of a 'falling
dominoes' sequence.

117 *nec*: for *neve* or *neu* (GL 270 note, W 128.iii). * *civil-*

ibus: 'domestic', 'family' (cf. 118 *fratribus*, 123 *fratres*). Cadmus is an outsider and must not poke his nose in.

119 *iaculo cadit*: 'he is felled by a spear', instrumental abl. (*cadit* = *caeditur*: GL 214.1). * *eminus*: a brachylogy for (*iaculo*) *quod eminus immissum est* (cf. Sallust, *Jugurtha* 101.4 '*ceteri* ... *ab iaculis eminus emissis corpora tegere*'). The basic meaning of the adv. is 'out of hand's reach' (opp. *com-minus*), so 'at, from a (spear-throw's) distance'. * *ipse*: 'in his turn'.

120 *hunc* ... *illo*: both refer to the same man, the *ipse* of 119. *quoque* attaches the whole sentence - 'Next, ... '. * *longius*: for *diutius*, with abl. of comparison.

121 *modŏ*: adv. with *acceperat*.

122 *exemplo pari*: 'in like fashion'. *par* commonly approximates to *idem*, with which it is often coupled (e.g. Cicero, *Pro Murena* 21 '*quem ego* ... *pari atque eadem in laude ponam*').

122 - 123 *suo Marte*: 'in combat with each other' (cf. *mutua vulnera*); *suo* = *inter se*. The phrase is a variation on *bello civili* (117), *Mars* being a metonymy for *bellum*, like *Liber* or *Bacchus* for *vinum*, *Ceres* for *fruges* or *frumentum*.

123 *subiti*: 'fast-appearing' with a play on one literal sense of *subire*, 'to sprout' (cf. *Georg.* 1.180 '*ne subeant herbae*' and note *seges* 110 above).

125 A Golden Line of the abVBA or 'enclosing' type; see on 74 above. * *tepido pectore*: abl. of description, making a second epithet for *matrem* (i.e. the earth): *tepido* is explained by *sanguineam*. * *plangebant*; 'smote in death'; cf. *Her.* 16.336 '*caesaque sanguineam victima planget humum*'.

126 *quinque superstitibus*: abl. absolute, 'there being five survivors', 'leaving five'; cf. GL 410 note 5, K 237, W 50. * *Ĕchīōn*: the name means 'Snakeman'. The other four were Udaeus ('Groundman'), Chthonius ('Earthman'), Hyperenor ('Overbearing') and Pelorus ('Monster'); see Introduction p. 15.

127 *Tritonidis*: *Tritonis*, an epithet of Athene, is to be connected either with the river Triton in Arcadia or with Lake Tritonis in N. Africa. It may commemorate the goddess' origins as a water divinity, though there is no trace of this in the surviving myths about her (Rose

(1958) 108 f.).

128 *fidem pacis petiitque deditque*: 'exchanged a pledge of
peace'; cf. *Aen.* 8.150 *'accipe daque fidem'* (following
Ennius, *Annales* 78). For *-que ... -que*, see on 7 above.

129 *operis comites*: predicative, 'as fellow workers'; the
gen. is perhaps better regarded as partitive (GL 374,
W 73.3) than objective (similarly 147 *participes operum*, 259 *generis socii*). * *Sidonius hospes*: an epic
periphrasis, the epithet indicating Cadmus' origin
(Sidon stands by synecdoche for Phoenicia) and the noun
his present status (cf. 24 - 5).

130 *cum posuit*: a pure temporal clause with indic., 'at the
time when (that) he built'; *cum poneret* would super-
impose the notions of circumstance and intention on
that of point of time (GL 580, K 434 (a), W 232).
* *sortibus*: instrumental abl. qualifying *iussam*.

Actaeon, 131 - 252

131 *iam*: as often, marks a new section of the narrative (cf.
1, 50, 144, 1.253, 6.486 etc.), here the transition to
Actaeon. * *stabant*: 'stood finished'; cf. Livy 6.4.6
'intraque annum nova urbs stetit.' * *poteras*: 'you
might have'; for the mood, see GL 597.3a, K 441 (b),
W 200.i on conditional sentences. This however seems
a true potential sentence, requiring no protasis (*si*
clause) to complete the sense; *poteras* therefore is
the equivalent of an imperfect subjunctive suggesting
what was likely to happen in the past, not of a plu-
perfect subjunctive, which very rarely expresses pot-
entiality in the past (GL 258, W 118; cf. on 62 above).
* *Cadme*: apostrophes of this kind are, in Ovid, largely
a matter of metrical convenience; cf. 1.438, 720, 728,
2.176, 543, 677 (at 140 below, Ovid even addresses Actaeon's hounds). Earlier epic employs them sparingly
and for special effect. Later the device tends to become an irritating mannerism (especially in Lucan).
Rhetorical conventions are responsible.

132 *exilio felix*: an oxymoron (cf. 5), that corresponds, anti-
thetically, to *poenam ... exilium* in 4 - 5 and so draws
the threads of the Cadmus episode together at its close.
The abl. is one of respect. * *soceri*: 'in-laws', both
father and mother; cf. *Aen.* 2.456 - 7 *'Andromache ferre
incomitata solebat/ad soceros et avo puerum Astyanacta
trahebat'*. Similarly *pueri* may denote male and female

children, *fratres* brother and sister.

133 *huc adde genus*: lit. 'add to this your descendants', so
'furthermore (there were) ... ' *genus* is defined by
and subdivided (alliteratively) into *natas, natos* and
nepotes. * *de coniuge tanta*: Harmonia, whose divine
parentage explains the epithet. For *de* of human origin, cf. 260 - 1 and *Aen.* 9.697 '*Thebana de matre noth-
um Sarpedonis alti*'.

134 *pignora*: cf. Propertius 4.11.73 (a dead wife addresses
her husband) '*nunc tibi commendo communia pignora
natos*'. Any close relative may be described as a
pignus (sc. *amoris*), though children are most often so.

135 *iuvenes*: 'grown-up'. * *scilicet*: not here ironical,
but asserting the truth of an observation.

135 - 136 *ultima* ... *debet*: 'for mankind it is necessary to
wait for the last day (of a man's life), and no one
ought to be called happy before he's dead and buried.'
The second half of this *sententia* elucidates and amplifies the first; Ovid does not mean in 135 that men
must expect each day to be their last, which would be
entirely irrelevant to Cadmus' situation. The thought,
that true happiness cannot be attained in life, was
an ancient commonplace; e.g. Herodotus 1.32.7, where
Solon advises King Croesus that, even in the case of
the well-to-do and healthy, πρὶν δ' ἂν τελευτήσῃ, ἐπι-
σχεῖν, μηδὲ καλέειν κω ὄλβιον ἀλλ' εὐτυχέα ('we must
reserve judgement before he is dead, and not call him
blest, but only lucky'). *homini* makes much better
sense as a dat. of reference or (dis)advantage (GL 350,
K 221, W 64, 65 and 202 *ad fin.*) than as dat. of agent
with the gerundive.

137 *suprema funera*: poetic pl., 'last rites' (= *exsequiae*).
supremus is often used of death or what is associated
with it.

138 *nepos*: i.e. Actaeon, the son of Cadmus' daughter Autonoë.

139 - 140 *cornua addita*: 'the addition of horns'; the English
idiom is abstract where Latin prefers the concrete use
of the past part. pass. (GL 437 note 2, K 393, W 95
and 96).

140 *sanguine erili*: instrumental abl. *erili* = *eri*; Latin
frequently substitutes an adj. for the gen. (possessive) of the related noun; so *nomen regium* = *nomen regis*,
humana consilia = *hominum consilia*, etc.; cf. 308, 722).

141 *at*: 'yet', conveying indignation or sorrow: Actaeon did
   not deserve such a fate, for he was guilty not of a
   crime but of a misdemeanour, and that was Fortune's
   fault (*Fortunae crimen*). The story of Actaeon as told
   by Ovid follows the version most widely current in the
   Hellenistic period (Apollodorus 3.4.4). Others existed:
   first, that Actaeon paid court to Semele and was destroyed by Jupiter out of jealousy (Acusilaus, after
   Hesiod); secondly, that he claimed to be a better hunter
   than Diana, for which he was punished in the way described here (Euripides, *Bacchae* 337 ff.); thirdly,
   that he sought to marry Diana, with the same consequences (Diodorus 4.81.4). Ovid probably drew on one (or
   perhaps more than one) Alexandrian short epic or epyllion, from which he took the main outline of the tale
   and the names of the dogs (his list differs from Hyginus' or that interpolated in some Mss. of Apollodorus).
   But whereas in his source Actaeon seems to have been a
   Peeping Tom who got his just deserts, Ovid represents
   him as an unwitting intruder, punished with quite dis-
   proportionate severity by a prudish and sadistic Diana.
   The model for this innocent Actaeon is Tiresias in Callimachus' *Bath of Pallas* (*Hymn* 5), who likewise was unfortunate enough to stumble across a goddess bathing.
   Athene is there as lenient with Tiresias as she was
   allowed to be by divine law, blinding him but giving
   him the gift of prophecy in compensation (cf. the explanation given at 333 ff. below). Ovid's Diana stands
   at the opposite moral pole to Callimachus' Athene.

141 - 142 *si quaeras, invenies*: a fut. indic. is regular in
   the apodosis of generalising ideal conditions (GL 596.1,
   W 195).

142 *quod ... habebat*: 'for what crime was involved in going
   astray?'

143 *mons erat ...* : a typical formula for the start of an
   ecphrasis (see on 28 - 34 above). But the description
   is not developed and gives way instead to a combination
   of two other standard paragraphing devices, a reference
   to the time of day (see on 50 above) and *iam(que)* + inverted *cum* (see on 1 - 3 above). Nor does any adverb
   of place correlative with *mons* appear. In view also
   of the elaborate ecphrasis of the *vallis Gargaphie* just
   below (155 ff.) it is possible that 143 represents the
   ghost of an alternative version that Ovid intended to
   reject. The *mons* is Cithaeron, south of Thebes (cf.
   702 ff.). * *caede*: for *sanguine* by metonymy (cause
   for effect).

145 A variation on 144. *ex aequo distabat*: 'was equidistant

from'. * *meta utraque*: abl. of separation. Two *metae*,
each a group of conical pillars, stood at the ends of
the *spina* or central reservation in the Roman *circus*
round which the competing chariots raced; one served
as the winning post, usually after seven laps. The
sun-god in Graeco-Roman mythology, like the moon and
(sometimes) dawn, was conceived as travelling across
the heavens in a chariot drawn by four or two horses
(2.153 ff.).

146 - 147 *placido ore*: 'in gentle tones', 'softly' (abl. of
manner).

146 *lustra*: the primary meaning of *lustrum* is 'mud' or 'mire'
(cf. *lutum*) - hence 'rough place', 'haunt of wild animals', 'forest'; cf. *Aen*. 3.645 - 6 '*vitam in silvis
inter deserta ferarum/lustra domosque traho*'.

147 *Hyantius*: adj. formed from *Hyas*, eponymous ancestor of
the Hyantes, an aboriginal Boeotian tribe mentioned
by Greek writers and by the elder Pliny. The choice
of a learned and recondite instead of a familiar epithet
is a typical 'Alexandrian' touch. Ovid does not, however, go to extremes in this respect.

148 *lina*: poetic synonym of *plagae*, large nets made of knotted rope (cf. 154 *nodosa*) and fastened between trees,
into which game was driven.

149 *satis*: adv., 'in sufficient measure'. * *altera*: 'another', i.e. 'tomorrow's' (= *crastina* or *postera*).

150 *croceis invecta rotis*: cf. *Aen*. 12.76 - 7 '*cum primum
crastina caelo/puniceis invecta rotis Aurora rubebit*'.
rotis = *curru* by synecdoche. *croceus* and *puniceus*
both render, imperfectly, the Homeric adj. for dawn,
ῥοδοδάκτυλος ('rosy-fingered'). The colour of the
flower called *crocus* (*Crocus sativus*) is reddish-
purple. (The spice saffron prepared from its dried
stigmas is yellow, which *croceus* sometimes means, but
not in a context like this.)

151 - 152 *utraque distat idem meta*: Actaeon's words echo those
in the narrative (145), an ingenious imitation by Ovid
of Homer's formulaic method of composition, with the
added sophistication of reversed word order. *idem* (n.)
is accus. of extent in space (GL 335, K 282, W 10);
it corresponds to *ex aequo* above.

152 *vaporibus*: 'its burning rays'. The second half of the
line is a variation on *Phoebus utraque meta idem distat*; but in reality the hunters are in the woods, out

of sight of *arva*, and screened from the *vapores*.

154 *intermittuntque laborem*: the line suddenly slows to a
crawl after the caesura with the heavy, polysyllabic
verb. Rhythm is matched to and assists sense: Actaeon's
orders are quickly executed, then comes the siesta.

155 *piceis*: the pitch-pine (*Picea excelsa*), a tree typical
(in poetry) of remote, dense forests. * *acuta*: lit.
'pointed', qualifying both *piceis* and *cupressu* (it
is a standard principle in verse that an epithet in
this position and relationship be taken with *both*
nouns; see Kenney (1973) 130 f.). 'Sharp(-leaved)'
makes an excellent epithet for any species of pine with
needles (cf. e.g. 1.699), but does not suit the cypress.
Either Ovid has been a little careless, or we are to
interpret the adj. differently with *cupressu*, as 'taper-
ing'.

156 *Gargaphie*: there was a spring of this name near the Boeotian town of Plataea, on the road to Megara; Pausanias
(9.2.3) calls it simply Actaeon's spring. Ovid's topography, however, is fictitious; he imagines a valley,
named after the spring, running back into Mount Cithaeron (see on 143 above), on which Actaeon's death was
traditionally placed (Apollodorus 3.4.4). The 'real-
ism' of the scene is a matter, not of observation, but
of literary convention. * *succinctae*: the tunic (*tun-
ica*, χιτών) could be shortened by gathering and tying
it at the waist (*succingere*), to facilitate movement
when ploughing, hunting, etc. Diana the huntress is
habitually represented in such a costume, with her
knees and lower legs bare - e.g. the 'Diana of Ver-
sailles' in the Louvre.

158 - 159 *simulaverat artem ingenio natura suo*: the Romans,
by and large, disapproved of nature untamed by man.
Wealthy individuals took delight in creating improved,
more comfortable, idealised versions of natural land-
scapes in the gardens of their country houses: arbours
and grottoes with running water, marble furniture instead of rocks, trained trees, etc.; cf. Horace, *Odes*
1.5.3, the pseudo-Virgilian *Copa* 7 ff., Seneca, *Epistulae* 5.6.39 - 40. Here, nature is congratulated
(ironically) for having managed by her own unaided
genius to imitate a man-made bower of this kind. (Pre-
Romantic English taste of the 18th century was not dis-
similar - e.g. the gardens at Stourhead, Wiltshire.)

160 *nativum duxerat arcum*: 'had raised a natural arch'. *pumice* and *tofis* are abl. of material (GL 396.3, W 40.3
and note i).

162 *margine* ... *hiatus*: lit. 'girdled as to its broad pools
with a grassy border'. *patulos hiatus* is acc. of respect denoting the part of the body concerned (GL 338,
K 213, W 19.ii), the pools being thought of as part
of the *fons*. Latin poets are fond of this Greek construction (cf. 221). The acc. of respect is also used
after a simple adj., e.g. 9.307 *'flava comas'* or *Aen.*
5.97 *'nigrantes terga iuvencos'*.

163 *dea silvarum*: Diana (Artemis) is the goddess of wild
life, both its destroyer and its protector, perfectly
reconcilable functions. This is perhaps her most ancient aspect, developed from the Minoan cult of the
'Lady of the Beasts' (πότνια θηρῶν), and associated
particularly with Arcadia's wild and forested uplands.
Diana's other roles, which have different cult origins,
include moon goddess and goddess of childbirth; see
Callimachus, *Hymn* 3, Apollodorus 1.4.1 ff. and Rose
(1958) 112 - 22.

164 *rore*: an elevated synonym of *aqua*.

165 *quo*: this, not *hic* at 163, marks the return to the story
after the ecphrasis.

166 *armigerae*: in apposition to *uni* ('to one, her squire ... ').
* *retentos*: 'unstrung'. Diana's attendant nymphs
(twenty for the chase, according to Callimachus) each
have their specialised tasks: one takes her cloak, two
remove her footwear, one does her hair, five bath her,
etc. The picture makes one think of a Roman lady's
formal toilette in her boudoir, surrounded by *ancillae*.
The incongruity with the surroundings is deliberate
and humorous. Contrast the natural simplicity of
Diana's ablutions in 2.454 ff.

168 *vincla*: the thongs or laces of Diana's hunting boots
(*coturni*, κόθορνοι); cf. *Ecl.* 7.32 (also of Diana)
'puniceo ... suras evincta coturno'. * *nam doctior
illis*: explains why Crocale ('Pebble') has the superior
job of coiffeuse (*ornatrix*). The phrase should logically follow *Crocale* (169).

169 *Ismenis*: a patronymic, 'daughter of Ismenus', a Boeotian
river. Ovid uses the pl. *Ismenides* generically for
'the women of Thebes' (e.g. 733).

170 *nodum*: plaits gathered and pinned in a knot or bun at
the back of the head. * *erat*: indic. with *quamvis*
is found in poetry from Lucretius on, in prose from
Varro (GL 606 note 1, K 447 note 1). * *solutis*: sc.
capillis, abl. of description.

171 - 172 A brief catalogue (see also on 206 ff. below).
Roman poets were greatly attracted by the exotic and
beautiful sounds of Greek proper names, which is one
reason for such lists as this. These nymphs of the
bath appropriately all have names connected with water:
'Cloud', 'Crystal', 'Raindrop', 'Drizzle' and 'Cup'.

172 *urnis*: instrumental abl. with *excipiunt*; either the same
or abl. of separation with *fundunt* (cf. W 42 note 2).

173 *Titania*: name or title of Diana, given because her mother
(Leto) and grandmother (Phoebe) were Titanesses; see
Rose (1958) 21 ff.

174 *dilata parte laborum*: 'having put off (doing) his share
of the work (of hunting)'. After his rest Actaeon
wanders off instead of resuming the chase with his
companions (243).

175 *nemus*: distinct from, but embracing, *lucus* (176). Servius, in a note on *Aen*. 1.314, provides the following
definitions: '*lucus est arborum multitudo cum religione*
(i.e. a sacred grove), *nemus composita multitudo arborum,
silva diffusa et inculta*'. * *non certis*: 'aimless'.

178 *sicut erant nudae*: 'naked, just as they were (sc. at the
time)'.

178 - 179 *viso viro*: abl. absolute.

180 *circumfusae*: middle, governing a dir. obj. (*Dianam*).

182 *collo tenus*: 'as far (down) as the neck', so 'by a neck'.
tenus also takes the gen. (though not in Cicero); it
always follows its case.

183 - 184 Diana's blush is likened to the colour of clouds
tinged by the light of *sol adversus* striking them,
or to 'rosy dawn'. To make the double simile fully
effective, the first comparison ought to be with
clouds at *sunset* contrasting with *sunrise*. Although
there are no parallels for *sol adversus* = 'setting sun',
the adj. nevertheless can be interpreted here in a
relative sense, 'over against the dawn', so 'westering'.
* *ab ictu*: an instrumental abl. with *a/ab*, meaning
'in consequence of', is not uncommon in Ovid (e.g. 571,
1.417, 2.601, 4.449) and is found even in prose, e.g.
Livy 2.14.3 '*inopi tum urbe ab longinqua obsidione*'.

184 *nubibus, aurorae*: dat. of reference (GL 350, K 221,
W 64). * *solēt*: the final syllable of the 3rd pers.
s. pres. indic. act. was originally long. Virgil re-
vived this quantity, but allowed it only before the

main caesura of the line, so that the lengthening is
aided by the syllable's carrying the metrical beat or
ictus; cf. *Aen.* 1.308 '*qui teneant (nam inculta vidēt),
hominesne feraene*' (3½ caesura). * *purpureāē āurorae*:
a spondaic fifth foot in the hexameter is no great rarity; the Neoteric poets of Catullus' generation affec-
ted it to a marked degree, Virgil much more sparingly.
The irregularity resides in the hiatus, a licence imitated from Homer and other Greek hexameter poets, Virgil once again being the pioneer in Latin. The particular pattern of line ending used by Ovid here (and at
4.535 *Ionio immenso*, 8.315 *Parrhasio Ancaeo*, 15.450
penatigero Aeneae, *Fasti* 5.83 *caelifero Atlante*) is
modelled on *Aen.* 1.617 *Dardanio Anchisae*.

185 The alliteration of *v* (= *w*) may be intended to have sin-
ister or unpleasant implications, but one cannot be
sure. It is very prominent in this passage: 189 *vultum
virilem*, 197 *velat vellere*, 200 *vero vultus vidit*, and
also 253 - 5.

186 *stipata*: supply *est*.

187 *in latus obliquum*: an adv. phrase, 'sideways on', 'turned
away'. Despite the protective screen of nymphs, Diana
modestly averts the front of her body from Actaeon,
whom she addresses over her shoulder.

188 - 189 *ut* ... *sic*: comparative, but (as often) with concessive force, 'though' ... 'yet' (GL 482.4, W 253 note
iii and 259). The indic. is normal with *ut* ... *sic*
(*ita*); *vellet* is an independent potential subj., 'she
could have wished' (GL 258, K 359, W 121), and is not
governed by *ut* as a true concessive conj.

189 *quas habuit*: with *aquas*; i.e. *aquas, quas (promptas) habuit, hausit*.

191 *narres*: dependent on the impers. verb *licet* (192); *ut*
is more often omitted than not after *licet, oportet*
and *necesse est* (K 417 note 1, W 124 note iii).

194 *dat*: for the compound *addit*; cf. *additus et* 198 below.

195 *spatium*: 'length'.

196 *cum pedibus manus mutat*: lit. 'she exchanges his hands
for feet'. The abl. without *cum* is more usual with
mutare in both verse and prose.

197 *maculoso vellere*: the 'dappled hide' of the fallow deer
(*Dama dama*).

198 Āutŏnŏeïŭs: a six-syllable adj. (two complete dactyls),
    formed from the name of Actaeon's mother, Autonoë.
    This formulaic type of periphrasis for a personal name,
    patronymic or matronymic adj. + *heros*, is metrically
    very convenient; e.g. 7.156 *Aesonius heros* (Jason, son
    of Aeson), 13.124 *Laertius heros* (Ulysses, son of Laer-
    tes). The line has the maximum number of dactyls to
    convey the impression of speed and thus aid the sense.

199 *cursu in ipso*: 'even as he runs'.

200 *ut*: temporal.

201 *dicturus erat*: virtually = *dicere conatus est*, the fut.
    part. denoting wish or intention; cf. 4.412 '*(Minÿeides)*
    conataeque loqui minimam pro corpore vocem/emittunt'.

201 - 202 *vox*: 'sound' in both lines, though plainly with the
    connotation 'human sound' or 'voice' in 201. Actaeon
    has acquired a stag's body, fleetness and timidity
    (198 *pavor*), but continues to think and feel as a man.
    The predicament of a human mind trapped in a non-human
    body is an aspect of metamorphosis that intrigued Ovid
    (and other poets before him); cf. 229 - 48 below, 1.630
    ff. (Io), 2.485 ff. (Callisto), 4.582 ff. (Cadmus), 11.
    734 ff. (Alcyone).

203 *non sua*: 'strange', 'alien'.

204 *quid faciat?*: a deliberative question (GL 265, K 407,
    W 172.2). The pres. subj. is put instead of the im-
    perfect for vivid effect, as if the action were taking
    place before the reader's eyes (*sub oculos subiectio*,
    repraesentatio); likewise *repetat* and *lateat*. * *domum
    et regalia tecta*: theme and variation. The second phrase
    identifies *domum*; Actaeon's home was his grandfather's
    palace.

205 *silvis*: local abl. without *in* (GL 385 note 1, W 51.iv).
    * *impedit*: 'prevents', 'vetoes'. Normally, when
    coupled like this, *hoc* = 'the latter', *illud* = 'the
    former'. It is doubtful, however, if Ovid meant that
    Actaeon was ashamed to lurk in the woods and afraid
    to go home; the converse seems more probable. So the
    reference of *hic ... ille* may be reversed, as it some-
    times is, (e.g. 1.697; GL 307 r.1). [Alternatively,
    pudor and *timor* may have become transposed in the text.]

206 *videre*: (sc. *eum*), for *conspexere*, 'caught sight of'.
    * *canes*: Ovid's catalogue runs to 19 verses (21, if
    we include 232 - 3) and lists 36 hounds in all, plus
    two unnamed ones (215 *natis duobus*). It is, in its way,

a *tour de force*, though critics both ancient and modern
have censured Ovid for not knowing when to stop in such
matters. This is one of several lengthy catalogues in
the poem: mountains feature at 2.217 - 26, rivers at
2.239 - 59, the islands of the Cyclades at 7.561 - 72
and trees at 10.90 - 105. Though the aural and antiquarian appeal of Greek names may partly explain Ovid's
predilection for such lists (though not the trees),
there are other reasons. The display of 'Alexandrian'
erudition is one, a puckish but affectionate desire to
outdo and parody the traditional epic (Homeric) and
didactic (Hesiodic) catalogue another. That Ovid's
excesses in this respect were calculated, not unwitting,
is shown by the tongue-in-cheek remark with which he
eventually curbs himself, *'quosque referre mora est'*.
Only a few lines later we find him unabashedly naming
a further three hounds.

208 *Spartana gente*: abl. of description, not origin (cf. e.g.
51, 223).

211 *cum Laelape*: instead of another nom., for variety; so
too 220 *Cyprio cum fratre*.

212 *pedibus ... naribus*: abls. of respect with *utilis* (GL
397, K 235, W 55); cf. 219 *cursu fortis* and 222 *hirsuta
corpore*.

214 *de lupo concepta*: lit. 'conceived from (a mating with) a
wolf'. The simple abl. or abl. with *ex* is also found
with *concipere*. * *pecudes secuta*: the phrase explains
or glosses *Poemenis*, which means 'Shepherdess'. Many
of the dogs' names are accompanied by an 'etymological'
description of this kind (in effect, a Latin rendering
of the Greek). Leucon (218) means 'Whitey', Asbolos
'Blackie', Aello (219) 'Storm-swift' (the name of one
of the Harpies in Hesiod, *Theogony* 267), Lachne (222)
'Shaggy' and Hylactor (224) 'Barker'.

216 *substricta ilia*: 'hollow flanks', a sign of good condition
in a hunting dog.

221 *medio frontem distinctus ab albo*: 'marked with a white
patch in the middle of his forehead' (lit. 'by middle
white', *albo* subst.). For the construction of *frontem*,
see on 162 above; for instrumental *ab*, see on 183 above.

224 *Argiodūs*: 'Bright-fang'. The *u* is long, representing
Greek ου (ὀδούς, -όντος, 'tooth').

225 *quosque*: for *et alii, quos. mora est* + infin. is a standard formula for cutting short a story. Others are

quid moror?, *ne multis morer* and *longum est*; cf. *Rem.
Am.* 461 *'quid moror exemplis, quorum me turba fatigat?'*.
* *cupidine praedae*: 'in their lust for prey', causal
abl. governing objective gen.

226 Three words for rock are brought together. Although they
denote different sorts of rock, distinctions in meaning
here matter very little; the verse is intentionally
pleonastic. The following line constitutes a variation
on it, *qua via difficilis est* picking up and summarising *per rupes scopulosque*, and *qua via nulla est* doing
the same for *aditu carentia saxa*.

228 - 229 *per quae ... ipse suos*: i.e. *per loca nota, per quae
famulos suos secutus fuerat, eos(dem) ipse fugit*. As
often, the antecedent, *loca nota*, has been drawn into
the relative clause; the object is common to both
clauses. * *secutus fuerat*: for the tense (replacing
secutus erat) see GL 250 r.1. *fugit* (228 and 229) is
historic pres. * *famulos*: 'servants', first applied
to an animal by Virgil - *Aen.* 5.95 '*(Aeneas) incertus
geniumne loci famulumne parentis/esse putet*' (the serpent that guards Anchises' tomb).

233 *haesit in armo*: 'latched on to his shoulder'.

234 - 235 *per compendia ... via est*: 'they stole a march on
the others by taking a short cut over the mountain'.
For *compendium* in this sense, Cicero uses *compendiaria*
(f.).

235 *dominum retinentibus illis*: abl. absolute.

236 The succession of *c* sounds suggests the snapping of jaws.

238 *possit*: potential. *quem non tamen = talem tamen qualem
non*.

239 *habet*: 'makes', 'utters' (governing *sonum*, 237).

240 *supplex similisque roganti*: a deer brought to its knees
by a pack of hounds is not of course supplicating its
hunters for mercy; it only seems to be. *supplici et
roganti similis* would be more accurate, but less pathetic. Anthropomorphic interpretation of animal behaviour was what in many instances gave rise to myths
such as the Actaeon story.

241 *tamquam sua bracchia*: almost = *pro bracchiis suis*, 'in
place of his (erstwhile) arms'. This, with *tacitos*,
focusses the horror of Actaeon's plight - unable to
signal his identity either by gesture or by speech.

242 *rapidum*: not 'swift' but 'ravening', i.e. tearing at the deer's flesh (*rapio*).

243 *oculis quaerunt*: i.e. *circumspectant*, 'look around for'.

244 *Actaeona clamant*: 'call on, shout for Actaeon', a less vivid but rhythmically preferable alternative to *'Actaeon!' clamant*.

245 *(ad nomen caput ille refert)*: another pathetic touch; the movement would not, and could not, be recognised for what it was by his companions.

245 - 246 *abesse ... capere*: the subject of the acc. and infin. is *Actaeona*, carried on from 244; *segnem* is predicative and emphatic, 'the lazy fellow'.

246 *nec ... praedae*: 'and not enjoying the sight of this heaven-sent prize'. *offerri* = 'to come one's way unexpectedly'.

247 *vellet*: past potential subj.; see on 62 *mota forent* and 188 *vellet* above (GL 258, K 359, W 121).

248 *fera facta*: 'savage attentions'.

251 *nec nisi*: after a neg. or virtual neg. *nisi* = 'except', without a finite verb. Here it introduces an abl. absolute equivalent to a temporal clause. Translate in the positive mode, 'and only when ... '

252 *satiata*: sc. *esse*, perf. infin. in nom. and infin. after *fertur* (GL 528, K 370). * Although a sequence of three lines with rhyme between adj. or part. at the caesura and noun in agreement at the end of the verse (250 *falsi ... cervi*, 251 *finita ... vita*, 252 *pharetratae ... Dianae*) is distinctly rare in Ovid's (or any other classical poet's) hexameters, this is insufficient cause to suspect the genuineness of 251 and 252. In every respect the lines are thoroughly Ovidian.

Semele, 253 - 315

253 *rumor in ambiguo est*: 'people expressed different views' (about Actaeon's death). The basic meaning of *ambiguus* is 'going this way and that' (*ambigo, -ĕre*, from *ambi* 'around' + *ago*), so 'changeable', 'uncertain'. (We need not enquire how or when it came to be realised that Actaeon had been transformed into a stag.)

* *aequo*: subst., abl. of comparison (GL 398, K 231, W 78).

255 *pars utraque*: 'each side'.

256 - 258 *non tam eloquitur* ... *quam gaudet*: 'so far from say-ing ... , she silently rejoices'. * *culpetne probetne*: a disjunctive or alternative indir. question. In prose *utrum* ... *an* or (-*ně*) ... *an* would be used (GL 461 - though cf. 460.2 note 2 - K 243, W 45). * *ductae*: 'de-scended from'.

258 *Tyria paelice*: 'the Tyrian trollop' (Brooks Otis), i.e. Europa.

259 *generis socios*: 'her kinsfolk'. *socius* often indicates relationship by blood or marriage. * *subit*: not 'is added to' (*accedit*) but 'takes the place of' (*succedit*). Juno's hatred of Europa is now supplanted by hatred of Semele, Jupiter's latest conquest; cf. *transfert* (*odium*) above.

260 - 261 *gravidam esse de semine Iovis*: 'to be carrying Jove's child'. *de* is causal; *per, ex*, or the simple abl. are found as well.

261 *Semelen*: although early incorporated into the Theban royal genealogy and given the Greek name Thyone, Semele was almost certainly in origin the Thraco-Phrygian earth-goddess, Zemelo. The name of her son was Diounsis in Phrygian (whence Diónysus). For the story of Semele's affair with Jupiter Ovid will have followed chiefly the *Bacchae* of Euripides (cf. 1 ff., 242 ff., 286 ff.). No Hellenistic poem is known. Cf. also the Homeric *Hymn to Dionysus* (7) 56 ff., Pindar, *Olympians* 2.25 ff. and see Apollodorus 3.4.3; Rose (1958) 149 f. (For the story that Semele was wooed by Actaeon - who may not then have been her nephew in that version - cf. Apollo-dorus 3.4.4, Pausanias 9.2.3 and see on 141 above). The figure of Beroë, Semele's nurse, whom Juno imperson-ates, is Ovid's own creation. The inspiration for her comes from *Aen.* 5.620, where the goddess Iris (*at Juno's behest*) assumes the form of an elderly woman called Beroë, one of Aeneas' band of Trojan refugees. In both Virgil and Ovid the supposed Beroë deliberately gives bad advice. The transition from *Actaeon* to *Semele* calls for all Ovid's skill as a narrator. 253 - 5 are there solely to pave the way for the introduction of Juno, who forms a third category of opinion contrasted with both the pro- and the anti-Diana groups. This technique of 'negative association' to link stories is one that Ovid uses a great deal in the *Metamorphoses*;

cf. e.g. 1.450 ff. ' n o n d u m laurus erat .../pri-
mus amor Phoebi Daphne', 1.583 ff. 'Inachus unus a b -
e s t .../... natamque miserrimus Io/luget', 7.515 ff.
'"multos tamen inde r e q u i r o ,/quos quondam vidi
... "./Aeacus ingemuit ... ' (there follows the story
of the plague at Aegina). While essentially artificial,
it is in general so deftly done that the reader does
not immediately notice its artificiality. * dum linguam ad iurgia solvit: 'while she gets ready to wax
abusive'(at her husband), lit. 'loosens her tongue for
reproaches'. For ad expressing the purpose or tendency
of an action see GL 416.1, K 285, and Lewis & Short
under ad I.D.3.b.

262 profeci quid enim per iurgia?: 'for what have I (ever)
achieved by abuse?' quid enim is postponed from the
beginning of the sentence; it does not have the same
force as quid enim? on its own, as at Horace, Satires
1.1.7 or Cicero, De Finibus 2.72. Aen. 5.850 perhaps
affords a parallel to the present passage, though editors tend to print the phrase in parenthesis, thus:
'"Aenean credam (quid enim?) fallacibus auris?"'

263 ipsa petenda mihi est: 'she herself must be my target'.
The reiterated ipsa ... ipsám (with variation of both
case and ictus) and the triple si ... si ... si ...
invest Juno's speech with a measured grandeur expressive of her haughty and calculating implacability.
The three conditional clauses, each increasing in
length (tricolon auctum), exhibit a climactic form of
theme and variation - maxima Iuno vocor (263), me sceptra tenere decet (264 f.), sum regina Iovisque et soror
et coniunx (265 f.) - but the climax is undercut by the
bitter qualification 'certe soror' (266), as Juno's
emotions begin to take control.

265 sceptra: a poetic or 'impressive' pl. As Queen of Heaven, Juno (Hera) is entitled to royal regalia. The
celebrated colossal gold-and-ivory cult statue of Hera
made by Polyclitus for her temple near Argos c. 420
B.C. showed her crowned and carrying a sceptre in one
hand, a pomegranate in the other (Pausanias 2.17.4).

266 at, puto: 'I suppose you'll say', 'no doubt it will be
argued that'. at introduces an objection anticipated
by the speaker. puto is heavily ironic; Juno knows
very well that Semele is not furto contenta.

267 thalami nostri: objective gen.

268 concipit; id deerat: 'she's with child; that's all it
needed!' (i.e. 'that's the last straw').

269 *quod vix mihi contigit*: Juno's only children by Jupiter
were Mars (Ares), Hebe and Ilithyia (Εἰλείθυια; sometimes however several Ilithyiae are mentioned, e.g.
Iliad 11.271). In addition she bore Vulcan (Hephaestus)
by parthenogenesis, after her husband had produced Minerva (Athene) from his head - a miraculous reproductive
tit-for-tat (Hesiod, *Theogony* 921 ff., Apollodorus 1.3.1);
see Rose (1958) 52 f. Juno's maternal resentment is
not surprising, for Jupiter's illegitimate offspring
were legion.

270 *uno ... vult fieri*: 'she means to become a mother by
Jupiter and by nobody else'. * *formae*: objective gen.
(GL 363.2 and note, K 262 (a), W 76).

271 *fallat eam faxo*: 'I'll see that he (Jupiter) disappoints
her' (ironically); less probably, 'that her beauty
(*forma*) cheats her'. Juno's stratagem is to make
Jupiter himself destroy Semele (so 'disappointing' her
of the joys of motherhood and especially of boasting
about the father). *fallat eam* is the 'theme', *ab Iove
mersa suo* ('her precious Jove') *Stygias in undas penetrabit* the 'variation'. *faxo*, from an obsolete *s*-stem
aorist of *facio*, serves as a fut.; it is a colloquial
form. For *facio (ut)* + subj., see on 13 above.

271 *Saturnia*: Juno was the daughter of Saturn (Cronos); cf.
173 *Titania*.

272 *mersa*: lit. 'drowned'. Semele, however, is consumed by
fire (308 f.), so the first meaning must be 'overwhelmed'
or 'destroyed'. But Juno intends a humourless pun, for
it is Jupiter's oath by the waters of Styx that causes
Semele's death and so her descent to the Styx.

273 *ab his*: 'after (saying) this' (= *post haec*). For this
temporal usage, frequent in Ovid, see Lewis & Short
under *ab* II.A.1. * *fulva recondita nube*: cf. *Aen.*
12.791 f. '*Iunonem* .../... *fulva pugnas de nube tuentem*'.

274 *nubes*: a purely metrical substitution for the s. *nubem* (cf.
nube in 273).

275 *posuit ad tempora canos*: 'arranged white hairs about her
temples'.

276 *trementi*: when used as an adj. the pres. part. usually
shows -*i* in the abl. (GL 82.1, K 74 note 1).

278 *ipsa erat Beroe*: 'she was Beroë to the life'. The local
adj. *Epidauria* confers on Beroë a certain solid identity.

279 *ergo*: 'well then', 'so then', resuming the thread of the
action from 224 *'limen adit Semeles'*; the main part of
the story is about to unfold. * *captato sermone*:
'having started to chat', for the more normal *incepto*
or *conserto sermone*. *loquendo*, abl. of the gerund,
though technically instrumental, nevertheless approximates to a temporal use of the past part. *locutae*,
'when they had talked for some time'.

280 - 281 *opto, Iuppiter ut sit*: indir. wish (GL 546, K 419 (a));
cf. Cicero, *De Officiis* 3.94 '(Phaethon) *optavit ut in
currum patris tolleretur'*. *opto* + infin. occurs more
in Silver Latin.

282 *thalamos iniere pudicos*: 'have gained access to chaste
girls' bedrooms'.

283 Having sown seeds of doubt in Semele's mind, Juno leads
her on towards her fatal request, the aim of which is
still to confirm that Jupiter is who he claims to be,
not to elicit some material gift from him (despite
donis, 309); *pignus* = 'proof' rather than 'token'.

284 *si modo*: 'if after all', qualifying the preceding statement; always with the indic. (GL 595 r.6). * *quantus
et qualis*: in their true form the immortals were of
gigantic size and incandescent.

285 *excipitur*: 'is embraced in love' (cf. 286 *complexus*,
284 *amplecti*).

285 - 286 *rogato det, ... sumat*: *ut* is occasionally omitted
in indir. commands even in classical prose; cf. Caesar,
De Bello Gallico 1.20.5 '(Caesar eum) *consolatus rogat
finem orandi faciat'*.

286 *ante*: adv., 'in your presence' (= *coram*).

287 *ignaram*: 'unsuspecting'. * *Cadmeida*: 'Cadmus' daughter',
Greek acc.; nom. *Cadmēïs* (GL 65 and 66.3, K 69 Proper
Names).

288 *formarat*: 'had moulded'. For the syncopated forms of
the pluperf. see GL 131.1. * *sine nomine*: adj., 'un-
named', 'unspecified'.

290 *quōque*: i.e. *et quo*, introducing a final clause containing
a comparative (GL 545.2, K 453, W 150).

290 - 291 For a god to swear by the waters of the Styx was to
bind himself by the most solemn of all oaths (e.g.
Iliad 15.38). Jupiter's unthinking promise to Semele

here is a double of Apollo's to Phaethon at 2.45 f.
and 101; in both cases love clouds judgment (exactly
as the shrewd Juno knew it would). For the explanation
of the Stygian Oath, and the consequences of breaking
it, see Rose (1958) 36.

292 *laeta malo*: an oxymoron, 'joyful at this calamity' (or
'calamitous utterance'); causal abl. * *nimium potens*:
'wielding too much power' (over her lover). * *peri-
tura*: 'destined to die'; the phrase glosses *laeta malo*.

294 *Veneris cum foedus initis*: 'when you make love'. *foedus*
is a standard term in love poetry for the sexual bond,
whether conjugal or not.

295 *da mihi te talem*: 'come to me thus'. * *ora*: 'lips'.

297 *neque enim ... potest*: lit. 'for neither is she (*haec*)
able not-to-have-wished, nor is he able not-to-have-
sworn', i.e. it is impossible for either to retract
their words.

298 *ergo*: consequential, 'accordingly' (contrast 279).

299 - 300 *vultu sequentia traxit nubila*: as Jupiter (Zeus)
was the god of the sky, the weather was naturally
thought to reflect his moods. In Latin this notion
first appears in Ennius, *Annales* 450 f. '*Iuppiter hic
risit tempestatesque serenae/riserunt omnes risu Iovis
omnipotentis*'.

300 *quis*: for *quibus*, dat. (GL 105 note 2, K 97), indir. obj.
of *addidit*. * *ventis*: dat. after *immixta*.

300 - 301 *fulgora, fulmen*: 'sheet lightning', 'bolt of lightning'; cf. Seneca, *Naturales Quaestiones* 2.57.3 '*eodem
autem modo fit fulgur, quod tantum splendet, et fulmen,
quod incendit*'.

302 *qua tamen usque potest*: 'yet as far as he can' (i.e. *quantum* or *in quantum potest*).

303 *centimanum Typhoea*: Typhoeus or Typhon was the most terrible of all Earth's offspring to challenge Jupiter,
who eventually managed to defeat and confine him (in
the underworld, in one version; beneath Mt. Etna, in
another). Hesiod, *Theogony* 823 f., gives the fullest
description of him: οὖ χεῖρες μὲν ἔασιν ἐπ' ἰσχύι,
ἔργματ' ἔχουσαι,/καὶ πόδες ἀκάματοι θεοῦ· ἐκ δέ οἱ
ὤμων/ἦν ἑκατὸν κεφαλαὶ ὄφιος, δεινοῖο δράκοντος ('whose
hands are possessed of strength, made for great deeds,
and untiring (are) the feet of the puissant god; and

from his shoulders rose a hundred snake's heads, those
of a dreadful dragon ... '). Ovid has changed the
heads to hands, thinking perhaps of the Hecatonchires
or Hundred-handed Ones, other children of Earth (cf.
1.183 f.); see Rose (1958) 58 ff.

304 *armatur*: middle (= *se armat*); see on 42 above. * *feri-*
tatis: partitive gen. after subst. *nimium* (GL 369, K
260, W 77.ii), like *saevitiae, flammae* and *irae* after
minus at 306 below.

305 *est aliud levius fulmen*: the thought that Jupiter keeps
two grades of thunderbolt in his armoury - 'heavy-duty'
and 'light-duty' (307 *tela secunda*) - is an amusing
fancy or *poetica licentia*, as Seneca describes this
passage (*Naturales Quaestiones* 2.44.1). * *dextra*
Cyclopum: the Cyclopes (s. *Cўclops*, Κύκλωψ), children
of Uranus and Earth, were the giant smiths who forged
Jupiter's thunderbolts beneath Mt. Etna (Hesiod, *Theo-*
gony 140 f. and 504 ff.; *Aen.* 8.416 ff.); making *dextra*
the subject focusses on their combined strength and
skill (cf. *Aen.* 8.452 f.). In Homer, however, they
appear as a race of primitive and unfriendly pastoral-
ists in Sicily (*Odyssey* 9.116 ff.).

308 *Agenoream*: adj. for the possessive gen. *Agenoridarum*
(or *-um*), 'belonging to Agenor's descendants'; see on
140 above.

308 - 309 *tumultus aetherios*: 'the celestial tempest' or 'thun-
derstorm'; for this special meteorological sense of *tum-*
ultus, cf. Horace, *Odes* 1.16.11 f. '*nec saevus ignis*
nec tremendo/Iuppiter ipse ruens tumultu'.

309 *donis iugalibus*: i.e. Jupiter's thunderbolts; the phrase
is ironic. Once more we have theme and variation in
308 - 9: *arsit* amplifies *non tulit*, while *dona iugalia*
and *aetherii tumultus* are related as cause and effect.

311 *si credere dignum est*: see on 106 above.

312 *materna tempora complet*: 'completes his mother's term'.
i.e. the time he should have spent in his mother's
womb - nine solar or ten lunar months; cf. *Ecl.* 4.61
'*matri longa decem tulerunt fastidia menses*'.

313 *primis cunis*: abl. of time when (GL 393, K 276, W 54),
'in his earliest babyhood'. *cunis* = *infantia* by metonymy. * *Ino*: one of Semele's three sisters; her story
is told in 4.416 ff.

314 *inde*: 'later', i.e. when he was older. * *nymphae*

Nȳsḗĭdĕs: 'the nymphs of Nysa', a mountain of uncertain
location, being variously placed by the ancient mythographers in Thrace, Thessaly, Macedonia, Syria, Egypt
and elsewhere.

Tiresias, 316 - 338

316 *dumque ... geruntur*: a Virgilian transition (e.g. *Aen.*
7.840 '*atque ea per campos aequo dum Marte geruntur*'
or *Aen.* 9.1 '*atque ea diversa penitus dum parte geruntur*'), though prosaic in type (Cicero, Caesar).
* *fatali lege*: abl. of cause, 'according to the dec-
ree of fate' (cf. 176, 348).

318 **forte**: introducing an anecdote (i.e. *memorant Iovem
forte ...*), 'once' or 'once upon a time', a very
common usage; cf. e.g. Horace, *Satires* 1.9.1, *Aen.*
3.22 and 9.3, Livy 1.24.1.

319 - 320 *agitasse remissos iocos*: 'to have joked idly'.
agitare = *agere*, *iocos agere* = *iocari*.

320 - 321 Direct speech introduced by a verb of saying that
is itself in an indirect construction (*dixisse*) is
perhaps restricted to Ovid; cf. 1.710 (Pan to Syrinx)
'*"hoc mihi colloquium tecum" dixisse "manebit"*'.

322 *placuit*: sc. *eis*, 'they resolved/agreed (to)'.

323 **Tiresias**: Tiresias has no direct connexion with the Agen-
orid line, but his great-grandfather was the dragon
killed by Cadmus. He is therefore a generation younger
than Actaeon and Pentheus, though he appears as an old
man (514 ff.). The version given by Ovid of how he
lost his sight and gained the gift of prophecy goes
back to Hesiod. An alternative, in which (like Actaeon)
he was punished for seeing what mortal eyes should not,
originated with Pherecydes and was popularised by Callimachus (see on 141 above). For further details, see
Apollodorus 3.6.7, Rose (1958) 195 f. * *venus utraque*:
'the two sides of love's coin', i.e. as experienced by
each sex.

324 *coeuntia*: 'coupling'; cf. 386 - 7.

327 *octavo*: sc. *autumno*.

328 *vestrae tanta potentia plagae*: 'such power in a blow
given you', i.e. 'if hitting you has such an effect'.

plagae is possessive gen. (GL 366 r.1, W 72.1.i);
vestrae is equivalent to an objective gen., 'yours' =
'suffered by you' (GL 364 note 2, W 74.ii).

329 *in contraria*: adv. phrase, 'into the opposite' (= *in contrariam sortem*).

331 *forma ... imago*: two ways of saying the same thing; *forma prior*, 'his previous shape' = *genetiva imago*, 'the fig-ure he was born with' (from *gigno*). *venit* and *rediit* are also virtual synonyms.

333 *firmat*: for *confirmat* (see on *posita* 1 above). * *iusto*: subst., abl. of comparison; see on *aequo* 253 above.

334 *pro materia*: 'in proportion to the subject'.

335 *aeterna nocte*: instrumental abl. of the penalty (GL 378 r.3, K 252 note 2, W 73.5 note iii).

336 - 337 *cuiquam deo*: dat. governed by *licet*. * *irrita fecisse*: 'to nullify', perf. infin. instead of pres. more for the sake of metre than for any other reason ('aoristic', 'archaising').

338 *scire futura dedit*: *do* + infin. in the sense of *sino* + infin. or *permitto*, *concedo ut* is first found in hexa-meter poetry in Lucretius, thereafter several times in Virgil; for its use by Ovid, cf. 1.485 - 6 '*"da mihi perpetua .../virginitate frui"*'.

Narcissus and Echo, 339 - 510

339 *Āŏnĭās*: a learned epithet for 'Boeotian'. The Aonian Plain formed part of Boeotia; it was named after an aboriginal tribe, the *Aones*; see also on *Hyantius* 147 above.

341 *fide*: 'trustworthiness', 'reliability'; gen. (GL 63 note 1, K 57 note 2). * *ratae*: 'certain', 'true' (lit. 'fixed by calculation'). * *temptamina sumpsit*: for *temptavit*, 'made trial of', 'put to the test'. Ovid employs a great many neuters in *-men*, *-minis*, which yield useful short syllables, e.g. *curvamen* (66) and (his own coinage) *moderamen* (567); see Kenney (1973) 126 f. Ovid resembles Lucretius in this respect.

342 *caerula Liriope*: the adj. (see on 38 above) is a common one for water nymphs. Liriope is not known from earlier

literature, but the part played by Cephisus establishes
the Boeotian provenance of the tale, and there is some
ancient evidence to connect it with the neighbourhood
of Thespiae, a village at the foot of Mt. Helicon.
For sheer beauty of sound and rhythm '*caērŭlă Lĭrĭ-
ŏpē*' is hard to beat. Partly the effect lies in the
reverse alliteration of the liquid consonants *l* and *r*
(-*RuL*-, -*LiR*-) and their own intrinsic sound values,
partly in the haunting quality of the vowels and diph-
thongs, partly in the delicate balance of the contrasted
hard consonants *c* and *p* at beginning and end of the
phrase. But the total effect is greater than the sum
of analysable factors.

343 *clausae*: 'enveloped', dat. (indir. obj.).

344 *enixa est*: for *enitor* trans. ('I give birth to') cf.
Aen. 7.320 '*Cisseis* (f. s.) *praegnas ignis enixa
iugalis*'.

345 *nymphis*: dat. of agent with pass. verb (GL 354, K 282
note 1). * *iam tunc*: 'even at that tender age' (sc.
'let alone when he grew up'; see 353 ff.).

346 *Narcissum*: the name is pre-Greek, like Hyacinthus, another youth who was turned into a flower (10.162 ff.)
or Cyparissus, metamorphosed into the cypress (10.106
ff.). * *an esset*: for *an* introducing a single indir.
question, see GL 460 note 1, K 406, cf. 405 note 2.

347 A Golden Line (AbVaB); see on 74 above.

348 *si se non noverit*: 'if he does not gain knowledge of himself' (fut. perf.). It has been suggested that Ovid
intended an allusion (no doubt cynical) to the 'motto'
of the Delphic oracle, γνῶθι σεαυτόν ('know thyself').
His Narcissus is a study of self-awareness leading un-
profitably to self-destruction, but it has no preten-
sions to philosophical depth, nor does it point any
very obvious moral. Narcissus exemplifies pure self-
hood or selfishness, just as Echo represents pure oth-
erness; neither condition is truly or wholly human.
For a full investigation of the Narcissus story and
its influence see '*The Narcissus Theme in Western Eur-
opean Literature up to the Early 19th Century*' by Louise
Vinge (Lund, 1967).

349 *auguris*: here, as often, a synonym of *vates*, 'seer'. An
augur was technically an interpreter of omens (lightning, behaviour of birds, etc.), not a clairvoyant.

349 - 350 *exitus illam resque probat*: lit. 'the outcome and

the event proved it (right)' (*illam* = *vocem*), i.e. 'the
way things turned out verified his prophecy'. *exitus
resque* = *exitus rei*, a hendiadys.

350 *novitas furoris*: 'the strange, unprecedented nature of
his passion'.

351 *ter ad quinos*: i.e. *ad ter-quinos* ('thrice five'), in
place of the flat and unmetrical *quindecim*. The order
namque ad ter quinos was available to Ovid but would
have entailed the loss of a valued dactyl.

352 *puer iuvenisque*: 'halfway between boy and man', i.e.
adulescens.

353, 355 Close imitations of Catullus 62.42 and 44 '*multi illum pueri, multae optavere puellae:/... nulli illum
pueri, nullae optavere puellae*', with the substitution
of dactylic verbs (*cupiere, tetigere*) for the spondaic
optavere; cf. also *Aen*. 11.518 f. '*multae illam frustra
... matres/optavere nurum*'.

354 *in tenera tam dura*: a cleverly juxtaposed antithesis;
furthermore the enclosing order of words (abBA) mir-
rors and reinforces the content of the line.

355 The consecutive clause expected after *tam dura* is replaced by a coordinate sentence without any connecting
particle (see GL 472.2 - parataxis). * *tetigere*:
'touched his heart', 'stirred his affections'.

357 *vocalis nymphe*: 'that talkative nymph' (cf. 358 *resonabilis*, 360 *garrula*). Throughout the *Metamorphoses*
Ovid prefers the Greek nom. *nymphē* to the Latin nom
nymphă. * *loquenti*: dat. of reference (GL 350.1, K
221, W 64 - Advantage), not found with *reticere* before
Ovid.

358 *Echo*: we first meet Echo as a nymph (an 'oread' or mountain nymph) in Euripides, *Hecuba* 1110 f., though she
is mentioned earlier by Pindar. Ovid is the only
writer to associate her with Narcissus; whether this
was his own idea or due to some Hellenistic source
cannot be determined, but, being a kind of auditory
reflection, Echo is ideally paired with Narcissus.
Elsewhere she appears as the beloved of Pan, who had
two daughters by her in one version, in another
failed to win her and in revenge caused her to be torn
to pieces by crazed shepherds, leaving only her voice.
* *resonabilis*: an 'etymological' epithet, like many
of those applied to Actaeon's hounds (214 ff.). *reson-
are* = ἠχεῖν, 'to echo, resound'; cf. also 496 *resonis*

vocibus.

359 - 360 *usum oris*: 'power of speech' (cf. 367 - 8).

361 *ut* ... *posset*: a noun clause standing in apposition to
    usum (GL 557 - Explanatory *ut*, K 415 (a), W 168), 'namely,
    the ability to ... '   *   *novissima*: 'last'.

363 *sub Iove suo*: 'under her husband Jove', i.e. in his em-
    brace.   There is a pun on *sub Iove* = 'under the sky',
    'in the open air', a standard meaning of the phrase.
    [The variant reading *cum Iove* is not as witty.]

364 *prudens*: 'deliberately'.   *   *tenebat*: for *detinebat*,
    'used to detain'.

365 *dum fugerent*: the subj. expresses design (GL 572, K 247,
    431, W 222).

366 - 367 Theme and variation again: *parva linguae potestas*
    more or less = *vocis usus brevissimus*.   Similarly in
    369, with chiasmus (V_1 A_1 A_2 V_2).

368 *re minas firmat*: 'she backs up her threats with action'.
    For this sense of *res*, cf. 350.   *   *in fine loquendi*:
    temporal, 'when(ever) one stops speaking'.

370 *ergo*: see on 279 above; verses 359 - 69 form an explana-
    tory digression.   *   *per devia rura*: 'in a remote part
    of the countryside' (repeated from 1.676).

372 *quo*: abl. of measure of difference with a comparative
    (GL 403, K 244, W 82).   The correlative *eo* is omitted
    before *propiore*.   With every step nearer her beloved,
    the flame of desire burns down nearer Echo's heart (or
    marrow).

373 *non aliter quam cum*: one of Ovid's favourite formulae for
    introducing a simile, particularly one contained in a
    temporal clause.   Virgil prefers *ac/atque* to *quam* after
    e.g. *non (haud) alius*.   *   *summis taedis*: dat. (*circum-
    lino aliquid alicui rei*).

374 *vivacia sulphura*: not 'long-lasting' (cf. 194) but =
    viva, 'lively', i.e. readily flammable and sparking
    freely.

375 *blandis dictis*: abl. of manner.

376 *natura repugnat*: 'her condition militates against this',
    i.e. she is physically incapable of it.   *nec sinit in-
    cipiat* rewords *repugnat*.

377 *incipiat*: the plain subj. after *sino* is mainly poetic
and occurs mostly after the imper. * *quod sinit*:
'what it (*natura*) *does* allow', in apposition to the
rest of the sentence.

378 *remittat*: final subj. (GL 630, K 453, W 148).

379 *forte*: 'as luck would have it'. * *seductus*: middle,
'having got himself separated'. Narcissus' situation
parallels Actaeon's (174 ff.). Isolation is dangerous;
there is safety in numbers. The classic case was that
of Hylas, the beautiful boy who went off on his own to
fetch water for the Argonauts and was dragged into the
pool by its amorous nymphs (Apollonius, *Argonautica* 1.
120 ff., Theocritus, *Idylls* 13, Propertius 1.20).

381 *aciem dimittit*: 'gazes about him'; *acies* (strictly 'keen-
ness of sight') is found in poetry as a synonym of
oculi from Lucretius on.

382 *vocat illa vocantem*: 'she calls to her caller'. The
echoic repetition of similar parts of the same verb,
in combination with the related noun (*voce*), suits the
sound of the line to the sense. Elsewhere Echo's re-
plies are quoted, not mimicked.

385 *alternae deceptus imagine vocis*: 'duped by the echo of
the answering voice'. The gen. is appositional (GL
361, K 248, W 72.1.5), i.e. the echo consists of the
answering voice.

387 *responsura*: best rendered by a relative clause, 'who would
never more gladly reply to any words'. * *'coeamus' rettulit*: in the eager Echo's mouth *coire* has the same
sense as at 324. All Narcissus meant was 'Let's meet'.
rettulit = reddidit.

388 *verbis favet*: lit. 'she promotes her words', i.e. suits
her action to them (by running to embrace Narcissus).
Others interpret *favet* as *gaudet*, 'she delights in what
she has said', but this seems pointless.

391 *emoriar*: fut., expressing defiance (an optative (wish)
subj. would require *utinam* with it). * *ante ... quam*:
like *postquam* and *priusquam*, *antequam* is often split
between the principal and subordinate clauses (GL 574
r.1, W 216). The subj. *sit* is final in type, denoting
intention (i.e. 'so that you may not have me') (GL 577,
K 432, W 227 and see on 365 above). * *copia nostri*:
lit. 'opportunity' or 'chance of me', so 'enjoyment of
me'.

392 Lacking *antequam*, the words turn into a pathetic prayer
(no longer final but jussive subj.).

394 *ex illo*: sc. *tempore*, 'thenceforth'.

395 *haeret amor*: 'her love persists' (lit. 'sticks to her');
cf. Cicero, *Philippics* 2.64 '*consumptis lacrimis tamen
infixus in animo haeret dolor*'. * *dolore repulsae*:
'through grief at being rebuffed'; causal abl. governing objective gen.

396 *tenuant*: poetic for the compound *attenuant*. * *vigiles*:
here with act. sense, 'that keep one awake'. *cura*
commonly signifies the mental torment of love; cf.
Lucretius 4.1059 f. '*hinc illaec primum Veneris dulce-
dinis in cor/stillavit gutta, et successit frigida
cura*'.

397 *adducit*: 'pulls tight', i.e. 'shrinks', 'shrivels up'
(= *astringit*); cf. *Georg.* 3.483 '*venis/omnibus acta
sitis miseros adduxerat artus*' (of diseased and emac-
iated animals).

397 - 398 *in aera sucus corporis abit*: lit. 'the sap of her
body evaporated into the air', so 'her body, once so
full of life, wasted away to nothing'. In Terence,
Eunuchus 318, Chaerea describes the girl he has fallen
for as having '*color verus, corpus solidum et suci
plenum*' ('firm and plump').

399 *manet*: 'remains unaltered'. * *lapidis traxisse figuram*:
'to have taken on the appearance of stone' - because
echoes usually occur in rocky places.

400 *inde*: temporal, 'ever since' (cf. 314). * *latet silvis*: repeated from 393, possibly a sign of lack of
revision. Some editors would eject 400 and 401, but
apart from this repetition they are unexceptionable.
Ovid, as is his wont, seeks to wring the maximum number
of points from his subject before leaving it: hence
the concluding, rather over-extended, play with Echo's
invisibility. * *nullo in monte*: a calculated allusion
to the fact that she was an Oread (see on 358 above).

401 *omnibus auditur*: dat. of agent with a finite verb (GL
354 note 1, K 222 note). *auditur* is antithetic to
videtur: though never seen, she is nevertheless uni-
versally heard. * *sonus ... in illa*: 'it is (only)
her voice that survives of her'. *in illa* cannot be
literally 'in her', as she has ceased to be corporeal;
rather it approaches *de illa* (partitive).

403 *luserat*: 'had made a fool of', 'deceived', by turning
out to be frigid and haughty; cf. *despectus* below.
* *ante*: 'earlier', i.e. when he was a boy and attrac-
tive, not to women, but to homosexually inclined adult
males.

405 *sic*: an idiomatic usage introducing a wish or prayer;
cf. *Ecl*. 9.30 '*sic tibi Cyrnaeas fugiant examina
taxos*', Horace, *Odes* 1.3.1 ff. '*Sic te diva potens
Cypri,/sic fratres Helenae, lucida sidera,/ventorumque
regat pater*'. The anaphora of *sic* lends intensity and
also helps to balance the two clauses formally just as
they are balanced in terms of content (*amet* is picked
up by *amato*; see on *vocat ... vocantem* 382 above).

405 *amato*: either the abl. or the gen. is correct with *pot-
ior* = 'I gain possession of', 'get hold of'.

406 *dixerat*: not the ubiquitous epic formula for marking the
end of a speech (e.g. *dixit (et)*, *haec ubi dicta*), but
belonging with the direct speech and parallel to *luserat* (403). * *Rhamnusia*: a title of Nemesis, 'the
affliction-bringing daughter of Night' (Hesiod, *Theogony* 223 f.), who was worshipped as goddess of retri-
bution or justice at Rhamnus on the north-east coast
of Attica. Her cult statue, by Agoracritus of Paros,
a pupil of Phidias, was carved from a block of Parian
marble (see on 419 below) allegedly brought with them
by the Persian invaders of 490 B.C.

407 - 413 The third of the ecphrases in the book. The emphasis is on (a) the secret, (b) the inviting nature of
the spot. Ovid's description is carefully structured
using a combined pattern of 2 and 3 units marked off
by anaphora: the major divisions are signposted by *quem
... quem*, and each relative clause is given three subjects. In the first clause *neque ... neque* connects
subjects 1 and 2 (*pastores, capellae*); in the second,
subjects 2 and 3 (*fera, ramus*) are linked by *nec ...
nec*. *-ve* and *nulla* (409) are each variants for a further *neque*. The effect of all this unobtrusive syntactical artistry is to produce a sense of ordered
calm that reinforces the verbal picture. By now the
reader is prepared for such idyllic scenes to become
the backdrop to some frightening or violent act.

409 *contigerant*: 'had come across', 'visited', with the under-
lying notion of disturbance or even defilement by drink-
ing (cf. the common meaning of the past part. pass.
contactus, 'polluted'). This notion surfaces in *turbarat* (410).

412 *passura*: 'which would always ensure that ... not'. The
fut. part. brings out the changelessness of the scene
in a way that the past part. *passa* could not.

413 *hic*: adv., with *procubuit*.

414 *faciemque loci fontemque secutus*: 'drawn on by the appearance (i.e. beauty) of the place and by the (? sound
of the) spring'.

415 *altera*: 'another, different kind of', i.e. *alia*. For
sitis = *cupido, furor amatorius* cf. Lucretius 4.1097 ff.
(a very powerful simile) and *Rem. Am.* 533 '*explenda
est sitis ista tibi, qua perditus ardes*'. The theme
of 415 is elaborated in the following verse and a half.

416 *correptus*: 'arrested', 'fascinated'.

417 *spem sine corpore*: the prep. phrase stands for an adj.,
'insubstantial'; cf. *sine crimine* 551 below. *spes*,
like English 'hope', may denote that in which one's
hopes are placed, whether persons or things. * *amat*:
'falls in love with'. * *corpus* ... *unda est*: the explanation seems at first sight an oddly condescending
and unnecessary comment for the narrator to make; but
there are others of the same kind to come (425 *imprudens*, 430 *quid videat, nescit*), which, together with
the culminating apostrophe to Narcissus in person
(432 - 7), add up to a deliberate strategy on Ovid's
part - to create pathos. We are invited to shake our
heads sadly over the simple-mindedness of the poor
youth. Narcissus' mental state is very cleverly con-
veyed; the syntax reflects the actuality as closely
as is possible in a string of active/passive correspondences - 424 *miratur/mirabilis est*, 425 *probat/pro-
batur*, 426 *petit/petitur*, *accendit/ardet* (= *accenditur*).
These correspondences catch the paradoxical and (literally) mirror-image quality of events. One may however begin, here if anywhere, to share the elder Seneca's
opinion (*Controversiae* 9.5.17) that Ovid '*nescit quod
bene cessit relinquere*' (see on 206 above). Not content with charting Narcissus' reactions while ignorant
of what he is seeing, the poet at 463 ff. devotes a
further 20-odd lines to exploring his state of mind
after realisation. Clearly the psychological implications and dialectical potential of the tale fascinated
Ovid, and no doubt his audience too, but the modern
reader can be forgiven for becoming impatient.

418 *vultu eodem*: 'with unchanging expression'.

419 *haeret*: 'remains glued to the spot' (he is lying down).

* *ut ... signum*: the comparison is one of stillness, not colour, though the most famous quality of Parian marble was its whiteness (cf. e.g. Pindar, *Nemeans* 4.81 or Horace, *Odes* 1.19.5 f.). With Ovid's rather unimaginative and incongruous simile (the *signum* can hardly be lying flat), cf. Catullus' beautiful and effective one at 64.61 *'saxea ut effigies bacchantis'* (describing Ariadne, motionless, looking out to sea for Theseus).

420 *geminum, sua lumina, sidus*: an artistic, enclosing form of apposition (abBA), favoured by Virgil (e.g. *Ecl.* 1.58 *'raucae, tua cura, palumbes'*, *Ecl.* 2.3 *'inter densas, umbrosa cacumina, fagos'* and *Aen.* 6.842 *'geminos, duo fulmina belli,/Scipiadas'*), but commonest in the *Metamorphoses*. There are few parallels in Greek, although the patterning looks typically Hellenistic. *geminum* here = *duplex*, 'double'.

421 *et dignos ... , dignos et*: the first *et* connects 421 with 420; the second *et* is therefore not the second element in a 'both ... and' structure, but is either a single connecting 'and' or = *etiam*. The latter seems more likely, given the emphatic repetition of *dignos*: 'worthy of Apollo too' (whose looks were even more celebrated than those of Bacchus).

422 *colla*: a poetic pl., probably encouraged by the analogy of *cervices*, which is normally pl. in prose. The s. *collum* occurs at 428 below.

422 - 423 *decus oris*: 'his beautiful face'.

424 *quibus*: causal abl.

426 *pariter*: temporal.

428 *visum captantia collum*: 'trying to clasp the neck that he saw' (in the water). For *capto*, cf. Horace, *Satires* 1.68 f. *'Tantalus a labris sitiens fugientia captat/ flumina'*.

430 *uritur*: 'is fired with desire'; like *peto, accendo* and *ardeo* above, the verb belongs to the *sermo amatorius* or erotic vocabulary.

431 *error*: concrete, 'false/delusive image'.

432 *credule*: the tone is not contemptuous, but pitying. Ovid talks patiently to Narcissus as one would to a child that cannot comprehend a situation which to an adult is ridiculously simple.

433 *quod amas*: 'the object of your love', object of *perdes*.
The phrase is a native idiom, metrically convenient,
found earlier, e.g. in Terence, *Eunuchus* 309 and Lucretius 4.1061, and frequent in Ovid's love poetry.
* *avertere*: the imper. (here middle in meaning: 'turn
(yourself) away') replaces a conditional clause (*si
avertēris* or *si aversus eris*), to which *perdes* forms
the apodosis: 'if you turn away, you will lose ... ';
see GL 593.4 (example from Seneca), and Cato's proverbial '*rem tene, verba sequentur*' (= *si rem tenueris* ...),
or Juvenal 3.78 '*(Graeculus esuriens) in caelum, iusseris, ibit*' (= *si iusseris* ...). This type of parataxis
or avoidance of subordination (GL 472) lends directness
to the discourse.

435 *nil habet ista sui*: 'that (sc. *umbra*) has no substance
of its own'. For a similar partitive use of *sui*, cf.
Rem. Am. 344 '*pars minima est ipsa puella sui*'.
* *-que ... -que*: see on 7 above.

435 - 436 *discedet, si tu discedere possis*: a mixed condition
with an 'ideal' pres. subj. in the protasis and a fac-
tual fut. indic. in the apodosis (GL 596.1; see on 141 -
142 and 433 above).

437 *Cereris cura*: 'thought of food' (for the metonymy see
on *Marte* 123 above).

438 *opaca fusus in herba*: 'sprawled in the shady grass'
(*fusus* is middle, like *positus* above and *levatus*
below). *opaca* reminds the reader that the pool
is shaded by surrounding trees (cf. 412 and 441).
Actaeon's pool was similar (157-62).

439 *inexpleto lumine*: 'with never-to-be-sated eye(s)',
'hungrily'; abl. of manner.

440 *paulum*: adv. Narcissus has levered himself up on one
elbow (*levatus*) and turned his body so that he faces
away from the pool (cf. 474 '*ad faciem rediit male
sanus eandem*', when he turns back again to contemplate
his reflection).

442 - 443 *ecquis, ecquem*: artistic case-variation of the interrog. word in parallel questions (a form of anaphora).

442 *io*: an exclamation (1) of jubilation ('hurrah', cf. 728),
(2) of grief ('ah', 'alas'), (3) seeking to attract
someone's attention (e.g. 'hey', 'here', 'look'). Here
(2) and (3) are perhaps combined; cf. Tibullus 2.4.6.

'*uror, io, remove, saeva puella, faces*'. (At 4.513
'*clamat "io, comites, his retia tendite silvis"*' only
(3) applies.) Narcissus' appeal to the woods around
him illustrates a convention established in classical
tragedy and extended in Hellenistic poetry, whereby
the solitary lover confides his or her unhappiness to
some natural object. Originally women address the lis-
tening heaven or earth (e.g. Euripides, *Medea* 56 ff.,
Andromache 91 ff.; cf. Plautus, *Mercator* 3 ff.). Later
both men and women address trees or water or rocks or
other things; cf. e.g. *Ecl.* 2.4 f. '*(Corydon) haec in-
condita solus/montibus et silvis studio iactabat inani*',
Ecl. 10.9 ff. and 63, Propertius 1.18. Ovid's epithet
circumstantes (441) cast the woods in the role of att-
entive bystanders with - by implication - human facul-
ties (cf. 443 *scitis*, 445 *meministis*). * *crudelius*:
love and lovers are traditionally 'cruel' in the language of love poetry (e.g. 477 below, *Ecl.* 2.6, Horace,
Odes 4.10.1).

443 *latebra opportuna*: a collective s. (cf. 37 *urna*) in appos-
     ition to the subject.

444 *cum vestrae tot agantur saecula vitae*: 'since you have
     lived for so many centuries'. For the idiomatic use
     of the pres. tense in expressions of time where English
     demands the perf., see GL 230, K 105 (a) note 1. The
     gen. is possessive.

445 *tabuerit*: perf. subj., consecutive/generic (GL 625 r.2,
     K 452, W 230.3.a and b). * *longo in aevo*: abl. of
     time within which, expressing duration, + prep. (= *per
     longum aevum*) (GL 393 r.1 and 394 note 1, K 278 note
     3).

446 *et placet et video*: 'what I see delights me'. The verbs
     are then ingeniously repeated in reverse order (chias-
     mus), 'yet what I see that delights me, I find not'
     (i.e. 'I cannot touch'). *et ... et* is answered with
     precise formal symmetry by *-que ... -que*.

447 *error*: see on 431 above. * *amantem*: sc. *me* (not *omnem
     amantem*).

448 *quoque*: see on 372 above.

448 - 449 *mare, via, montes*: three traditional obstacles to
     lovers' union. City walls (*moenia*) are less expected
     in this context than house walls, behind which the
     beloved was confined by a jealous husband (a familiar
     motif of comedy and elegy); but then Narcissus' diffi-
     culties are hardly typical.

449 *clausis portis*: descriptive abl., not abl. absolute.

450 *exigua prohibemur aqua*: 'we are kept apart by a little
water' (instrumental abl.).

451 *oscula*: 'lips', puckered to bestow a kiss.

453 *putes*: 'one would think', potential subj., also known
as the subj. of 'conditioned futurity' (GL 257, K
359, W 119). * *amantibus*: sc. *nobis*. The sentence
is a variation on *'exigua prohibemur aqua'*. Two
thoughts dominate Narcissus' mind in 448 - 53: (1)
the barrier between himself and his 'lover' is neg-
ligible, yet insuperable; (2) his 'lover' wants physical contact as fervently as he does. He then starts
to complain about the other youth's unattainability,
which seems to contradict his responsiveness (454 -
462). Narcissus' puzzlement is summed up by the cry
'quove petitus abis?' (whenever he plunges his hand
into the water and obliterates the reflection).

454 *unice*: 'incomparable'.

456 *fugias*: consecutive subj. (see on 445 above). * *et ...
quoque*: attaching a second, more powerful argument.
In verse, and occasionally in prose too, *quoque* may
precede the noun it connects instead of following it.

457 *nescioquam*: quantitative, as often: 'some measure of'.

458 *cum porrexi*: frequentative *cum* (GL 584, K 434 (b), W 233);
similarly in 459. * *ultro*: lit. 'on the other side',
so 'in return' or just 'too'.

460 *nutu*: 'at my nod', 'when I nod' = *me nutante*, parallel
to *me lacrimante*, a characteristic syntactical *variatio*.
The abl. is temporal in type (W 54). (Alternatively,
but less satisfactorily, *nutu signa remittis* = 'you
return my signs with a nod', abl. of manner.)

461 *quantum suspicor*: 'as far as I can guess', a parenthetic
comparative clause. * *motu*: abl. of source or standard without *ex* (GL 402, W 41.5).

462 *aures non pervenientia nostras*: for the acc. of the goal
or direction without *ad* after verbs of motion, see GL
331, K 270, W 5 (v). The part. has the value of an
adj. and is best rendered by an adj. (relative) clause.

463 It is at this point that Narcissus 'knows himself', and
(as Tiresias predicted) his death follows. The discovery that the beloved is himself (*mea imago*) stimulates

a further self-pitying and self-dramatising flow of
elegant paradoxes and word-plays, which continues until the very end.

464 *flammas moveoque feroque*: *flammas moveo* = *amorem moveo*
(sc. *mihi*), *flammas fero* = *uror*. The second half of
the line thus forms a neat variation on the first.

465 *faciam, roger, rogem*: deliberative subjs. (GL 265, K
356, W 172 and 174). *rogare* here = 'invite', 'solicit',
'seek the love of'. * *quid deinde rogabo*: *quid* is
the internal obj. ('what invitation shall I make now?').
deinde rarely occurs in questions; cf. *Aen.* 5.241
'Aeneas "quo deinde ruis? quo proripis?" inquit'.
There are no good grounds for ever regarding *deinde*
as equivalent to *tandem* = 'pray', 'tell me' in interrog. sentences.

466 *inopem mè copia fecit*: a very clever oxymoron (cf. 5
and 132).

467 *o utinam possem*: a wish for the present (GL 261, K 357,
W 116). Hiatus is regular after the interjection *o*;
cf. *Am.* 3.1.16 *'o argumenti lente poeta tui'*, Horace,
Ars Poetica 301 *'o ego laevus'*.

468 *votum in amante novum*: 'here's a novel prayer for a
lover:' For this use of *in*, see GL 418.1b - Of Reference, and Lewis & Short, under in I.C. (near the
end). * *quod amamus*: as subst., subject of *abesset*.
For *velim, vellem* + subj. (indir. wish), see GL 271
note 2, K 419 (a) note 1, W 130 and cf. *'vellem diuturnior esset'* 472 below.

469 *iamque*: signals a new stage of the action; see on 1 - 3
and 131 above.

470 *superant*: 'are left', 'remain' (= *supersunt*), a good
prose sense; e.g. Caesar, *De Bello Gallico* 6.17.3 *'ea
quae bello ceperint plerumque devovent; quae supera-
verint, animalia capta immolant, reliquasque res in
unum locum conferunt'*.

471 *posituro*: tantamount to *quippe qui positurus sim*, giving
the reason why death is no hardship.

472 *diuturnior*: sc. *quam ego*. The adj. is rarely applied
to persons and is not found in poetry before Ovid,
who has to take a small quantitative liberty with it -
dĭŭ- instead of *dĭū-*.

473 *concordes*: predicative, '(being) in mental harmony',

'feeling the same about each other'. * *in una*: for
in una atque eadem; cf. *Aen.* 5.616 f. '*vox omnibus
una:/urbem orant: taedet pelagi perferre laborem*'
(Mackail's punctuation).

474 *dixit et*: one of many epic formulae for marking the conclusion of direct speech and the return to narrative
(see on *dixerat* 406 above). * *rediit*: 'turned back'
(to look at the water); since 442 he had been facing
the woods. * *male sanus*: i.e. *insanus*. *male* often
negatives laudatory or neutral epithets, whereas it
intensifies pejorative ones (e.g. *male fidus = perfidiosus, male perfidiosus = perfidiosissimus*).

475 - 476 *obscura reddita est*: 'was made unclear', 'turned
opaque'. * *moto lacu*: abl. absolute, instrumental
in function, 'by the disturbance of the water'. For
the idiomatic use of the past. part. pass. to express
an abstract idea ('disturbance', not 'having been dis-
turbed'), see on *cornua addita* 139 - 40 above.

478 *liceat*: sc. *mihi*. * *quod tangere non est*: 'what it is
not permitted (or 'possible') to touch'. *est* for
licet, in imitation of Greek ἔστι (for πάρεστι) + infin., is not attested before c. 50 B.C. (Mummius);
cf. Horace, *Satires* 1.2.101 f. '*Cois tibi paene videre
est/ut nudam*', *Aen.* 8.675 f. '*in medio* (sc. *clipeo*)
classis aeratas, Actia bella,/cernere erat'.

479 *misero furori*: 'for my wretched passion'. *misero = qui
miserum reddit*; cf. *Rem. Am.* 21 f. '*qui, nisi desierit,
misero periturus amore est,/desinat*'.

480 *summa deduxit ab ora*: Narcissus grasps the neck of his
tunic and rips it downward (hence *nuda pectora*, 491),
in a ritual gesture of grief.

481 *percussit pectora palmis*: the alliteration is partly
onomatopoeic (*p* and *c* being explosive sounds, like
slaps), partly emphatic.

482 *pectora percussa*: picks up in reverse order *percussit
pectora*. The phrase serves not only to connect the
sentences formally, but also to advance the action
(= *quae ubi percussit* or *quo facto*). * *roseum
ruborem*: pleonastic, but pleasingly alliterative,
like 'rosy redness' in English.

483 *non aliter quam*: see on 373 above. * *candida parte*:
either an adversative epithet phrase within the relative clause - '(though) white in part' - or standing
for *quae candida parte sunt*, coordinate with *parte*

rubent in adversative asyndeton. The extreme contrast
of red and white is a favourite with the Latin poets;
cf. Propertius 1.20.37 f. *'lilia ...∕candida purpureis
mixta papaveribus'*, *Aen.* 12.67 ff. *'Indum sanguineo
veluti violaverit ostro∕si quis ebur, aut mixta rubent
ubi lilia multa∕alba rosa'*.

484 *variis uva racemis*: 'grapes in many-coloured clusters',
abl. of description (*uva* is collective s.). For the
epithet, cf. Horace, *Odes* 2.5.10 ff. *'iam tibi lividos∕
distinguet Autumnus racemos∕purpureo varius colore'*.

485 *ducere*: 'take on', 'acquire'.

486 *quae*: the antecedent is *pectora* (482). * *liquefacta
rursus*: 'made clear again' (once the ripples have died
away).

487 *ut ...* : another simile (really two), hard on the heels
of the two previous ones. Such concentrations of
similes, often after long stretches without any, are
a legacy from Homer.

488 *igne levi*: 'with gentle heat'; it is the slowness of the
melting that Ovid wishes to bring out (cf. 490 *paulatim*).
* *cerae*: the pl. implies objects made of wax, e.g.
portrait masks, dolls, or displays of fruit and flowers.
flava is a standing epithet of *cera*; the items mentioned,
however, would normally have been painted.

490 *līquitur*: cf. *Georg.* 1.43 f. *'vere novo gelidus canis
cum montibus umor∕liquitur'*.

491 *rubori*: dat. of possessor (very rarely of non-human things)
(GL 349, K 224, W 63). *est = inest*. Narcissus' red-
and-white body (not his complexion; he has been pound-
ing his breast and arms) now has no colour to it - the
first sign of dissolution. (The alternative explanation -
that *est = remanet* and that *rubori* is dat. governed by
mixto (abl.) - leaves the phrase *mixto candore rubori*
hanging in mid-air.)

492 *vigor, vires, visa*: emphatic alliteration of the most
significant words (cf. *color, candore* above). * *quae
modo visa placebant*: 'all the things which pleased him
when he saw them so short a time before'.

493 *nec corpus remanet*: Narcissus ends up sharing (more or
less) the same fate as Echo, whom he had spurned (cf.
494 *'quamvis irata memorque'*). Ovid very dexterously,
through this thematic link, brings her back into the
picture to enclose the Narcissus story in epyllion

fashion. Presently (511 ff.) Tiresias too reappears, thus completing the 'enclosing' structure of the middle section of the book; see Introduction p. 5.

496 *dixerat*: for the tense (frequentative; similarly *percus- serat* below), see GL 584, K 434 (b), W 233.

499 *spectantis*: sc. *viri* or *Narcissi*.

500 - 501 *remisit verba locus*: this amounts to an admission that echoes are produced naturally after all. Ovid the rationalist has rather naughtily 'pulled the rug out' from under his make-believe world, leaving it in doubt whether we should regard *Echo* at the end of the line as referring to the nymph or merely to the acous- tic phenomenon. It is quite unsurprising, however, to find Ovid writing of Echo a few lines later as if he had given nothing away. To allow rationalism more than a moment's freedom here and there would spell the end of the poem.

501 *dictoque 'vale'*: abl. absolute. The imper. is treated as an indecl. subst. * *'vale' inquit*: *vale* is scanned as a pyrrhic (◡◡) in hiatus before the initial vowel of *inquit*. Ovid has copied *Ecl*. 3.79 '*et longum "formose, vale, vale" inquit "Iolla"*'; cf. *Ecl*. 6.44 '*ut litus "Hyla, Hyla" omne sonaret*'. The fading of the second syllable of the echo is most ingeniously caught by this shortening (*correptio*). A second conjugation imper. like *vălē* tended in any case to be pronounced as two short syllables (e.g. *căvĕ*, *mănĕ*, *făvĕ*, *těnĕ*) owing to the phonetic law of *brevis brevians* or iambic short- ening; so the metrical licence is less than it might seem, though this does not detract from the subtlety of its employment in the examples quoted.

502 *viridi*: green is the colour of life and health (cf. *Aen*. 6.304 '*(Charon) iam senior, sed cruda deo viridisque senectus*'); Narcissus, by contrast, is pale and dying. The epithet is not a mere cliché; epithets seldom are in Ovid. The phrase *summisit in herba* is repeated from 23.

503 *mirantia*: equivalent to *dum mirantur*.

504 *inferna sede*: local abl. *inferna = inferorum*, 'of the dead'; see on *erili* 140 above.

505 *in Stygia spectabat aqua*: even after death Narcissus re- mained true to character - a witty touch. * *sorores*: see on 506 below.

505 - 507 *planxere, planxerunt, plangentibus*: the modified anaphora conveys the impression of the iterated noises of
grief that the words describe.

506 *sectos fratri posuere capillos*: 'cut off their locks and
dedicated them to their brother'. It was the custom
to crop the hair in mourning and lay it on the deceased's
grave. As Narcissus has not been buried, and in fact
leaves no corpse to bury, *posuere* cannot have quite
this literal meaning here. *fratri* is dat. of advantage,
'in honour of' (GL 350.2, K 221, W 64). Narcissus was
the son of a river god (342 ff.); hence by a slight
stretching of the facts all water nymphs (Nereids) may
be called his sisters.

507 *Dryades*: nymphs of oak (and by extension of other) trees.
    * *plangentibus*: dat. governed by *assonat* (an extremely
rare compound; here only in Ovid, and known from only
one earlier writer).

508 *iamque*: marks a later stage. * *quassas faces*: the past
part. pass. seems here to be a pure epithet with either
a timeless or a proleptic sense, i.e. either 'that have
been/are always shaken at funerals', or 'that they (prepare and then) shake' (see on *vitiatas* 76 above). Alternatively, the phrase means 'the shaking of torches',
though this does not go too well with *parabant*.
    * *feretrum*: a Greek loan-word (φέρετρον), synonymous
and cognate with pure Latin *ferculum*.

509 *nusquam corpus erat*: the abruptness of the asyndeton
(omission of a connective, here *sed*) matches the sudden-
ness of the surprising discovery. * *florem*: from
Ovid's description the flower can be identified as *Narcissus poeticus*, the Poet's Narcissus, a mountain species found from Spain to Greece. The *croceus flos* is
the red and yellow cup or corona of the flower, the
folia alba are the white perianth segments ('petals')
surrounding the cup (*medium cingentibus*). Ovid's bot-
anical vocabulary is derived from Virgil; cf. *Georg.*
4.271 ff. '*est etiam flos in pratis, cui nomen amello/
fecere agricolae .../aureus ipse* (i.e. *flos*, the central disc), *sed in foliis, quae plurima circum/fundun-
tur, violae sublucet purpura nigrae*'.

Pentheus, 511 - 581

511 *cognita res*: 'knowledge of the affair' (cf. 515 *lucis ademptae*), or 'when the affair became known, it ... '.

512 *nomenque ... ingens*: a variation on *meritam ... famam*.

514 *contemptor superum*: imitated from Virgil, who styles
Mezentius (*Aen.* 7.648) '*contemptor divum*'. At 1.161
Ovid has '*contemptrix superum*' of the race of men born
from the Giants' blood and typified by the impious
Lycaon. * Pentheus, cousin to Actaeon, succeeded
Cadmus as ruler of Thebes. Like King Lycurgus of
Thrace and the daughters of Minÿas (4.1 ff. and 4.389
ff.), he resisted the introduction of the cult of the
'new god' (520), and was punished for his unbelief.
The classic treatment of the Pentheus story was by
Euripides in the *Bacchae*, of which Pacuvius and Accius
had written Latin adaptations, the former entitled
Pentheus. Euripides does not seem to have been Ovid's
chief model, however. He may have consulted earlier
plays (*Bacchae, Pentheus*) by Aeschylus, of which only
a few fragments survive, but probably looked more to
Hellenistic poems, such as [Theocritus] 26, which gives
a description of the dismemberment of Pentheus very
similar to Ovid's in 721 ff., though it differs in
other, significant details. Cf. Apollodorus 3.5.2 f.,
Seneca, *Oedipus* 445 ff.; and Rose (1958) 152 f. For
Acoetes and the tale of the sailors, see on 573 and
582 below.

515 *senis*: see on 323 above. * *tenebras et cladem lucis
ademptae*: 'his blindness and the tragedy of his loss
of sight' (lit. 'light', a metonymy) - theme and
variation. For the idiom *adempta lux = ademptio
(amissio) lucis*, see on *cornua addita* 139 - 40 above.
The gen. is defining (appositional).

516 *obicit*: sc. *ei*; lit. 'casts it at him', so 'taunts him
with'.

517 - 518 *luminis orbus*: 'deprived of light', a poetic periphrasis for *caecus*. For the gen. with *orbus*, see GL
374.8, W 73.3. *huius* = 'that shines on us all' or
'that shines today'.

520 *novus, proles Semelēiǎ, Liber*: for the pattern of apposition, see on 420 above.

521 *quem ... honore*: 'if you do not deem him worth honouring
with places of worship'. *templorum* is a gen. of definition; cf. Tibullus 1.7.53 '*tibi dem turis honores*'.
* *fueris dignatus*: the 'periphrastic' fut. perf. denotes the completion of an existing state, rather
than of an action, in the fut. (GL 250; cf. *secutus
fuerat* 228 above).

522 The line is notable for its alliteration of *l* and *s*,
expressing perhaps bitter contempt.

523 *matremque tuam matrisque sorores*: i.e. Agave and her
two surviving sisters, Autonoë and Ino. For *-que* ...
-que, see on 7 above.

524 *eveniet*: not impers., but with *hoc* understood as subject ; 'this will come to pass'.

524 - 525 *neque* ... *-que*: for *non modo non* ... *sed etiam*, a
good prose usage; see Lewis & Short, under *neque* II.
B.4.a.

525 *tenebris*: the word throws back Pentheus' jibe (515)
in his teeth.

527 *dicta*: picks up *dicentem* (526) to connect a new section
of the narrative. * *fides*: 'belief' (cf. 341).
* *responsa vatis aguntur*: 'the seer's prophecies are
fulfilled'; cf. *Georg*. 3.491 *'nec responsa potest
consultus reddere vates'*.

528 *Liber adest*: cf. 102 *'Pallas adest'*. * *ululatibus*:
the ecstatic shrieks and howls of the worshippers
who are observing Bacchus' festival for the first
time (cf. 530 *ignota sacra*).

529 The first *-que* connects one sentence (*mixtae* ... *feruntur*) to the other (*turba ruit*); the second *-que*
is the first of a series and is not to be translated.

530 *vulgusquē*: the final syllable is scanned as heavy (or
'long'), because the initial consonants of *proceres*,
which for prosodic purposes are usually treated as
indivisible with the length of a single consonant,
have here (as it were) been split between the two
words, thus: *vulgusquep-roceres*. Single liquids like
l or *m* and other prolongable consonants like *s* are
also occasionally treated in this way in imitation of
Greek practice, found especially with τε. For a Virgilian parallel to the present example, cf. *Aen*. 12.89
'ensemquē clipeumque et rubrae cornua cristae'.

531 *anguigenae, proles Mavortia*: i.e. the Spartoi, one of
whom was Pentheus' father; cf. 95 ff. and see Introduction p. 15.

532 *aera repulsa*: concrete for abstract (see on 139 - 40
above), 'the striking together of brass cymbals'.
aes stands by metonymy for *cymbalum* (κύμβαλον), one
of the percussion instruments used in the orgiastic

worship of both Bacchus (Dionysus) and Cybele. The
other was the *tympanum* (τύμπανον: tambourine), mentioned in 527.

533 *adunco tibia cornu*: the Phrygian or Berecyntian pipe
(*tibia*, αὐλός) was a straight woodwind instrument played
with a reed, like an oboe, and having a curved, horn-
shaped bell something like that of a saxophone; cf.
Tibullus 2.1.86 '*obstrepit et Phrygio tibia curva sono*'.
This too featured in the worship of Cybele, the Asiatic
'Great Mother' goddess.

534 *magicae fraudes*: 'sorcerer's tricks'; cf. Euripides,
Bacchae 218 πλασταῖσι βακχείαισιν ('sham frenzies').
* *quos*: the relative clause precedes its antecedent
(*vos*, to be supplied as the object of *vincant*, 537).

535 *tuba*: the straight (Roman) war trumpet, as opposed to
the *cornu* or *bucina*. * *terruerit*: the subj. may be
generic, or have arisen by attraction into the mood
of the result clause (*ut ... vincant*). The verb is
positioned in the central one of the three phrases to
which it is common (*non ... , non ... , non ... ;*
double, anaphora with asyndeton).

537 *obsceni greges*: 'lecherous bands'. The sexual licence
attendant upon Bacchic revels appalled the outsider.
The *senatus consultum de Bacchanalibus* of 186 B.C. is
evidence of how alarmed the Roman ruling class was by
the threat to public morality and public order posed
by the spread of the cult from Campania; cf. Livy 39.8
ff. * *inania*: 'hollow', a standing epithet of *tympanum*, but having in Pentheus' mouth an additional,
special point - 'worthless', 'silly'; see on *viridi*
502 above.

538 *vosne, senes, mirer ... ?*: deliberative subj., asking a
question to which an answer is not expected or required.
These old men are the survivors of Cadmus' party from
Tyre. But it is clear from 46 - 9 that all the Phoenicians, excepting Cadmus himself, were killed by the
serpent. Through following different sources, or through
allowing his dramatic instinct free reign in the earlier
episode, Ovid has been led into inconsistency.

539 *hac*: supply *sede* and *posuistis* from the second member of
the sentence. For the Greek second declension acc.
Tyron, see GL 65, K 68. * *profugos posuistis penates*:
the adj. belongs especially to the vocabulary of the
Aeneas saga (e.g. *Aen*. 1.2, Livy 1.1.8). The whole
line is redolent of Virgil; cf. *Aen*. 1.68 '*Ilium in
Italia portans victosque penates*', 3.86 ff. '"*serva*

*altera Troiae/Pergama .../... quove ire iubes? ubi pon-
ere sedes?"'.*

540 *sine Marte*: 'without a fight'; see on *suo Marte* 122 - 3
above. * *vosne, acrior aetas*: sc. *mirer?* (538). Pentheus turns to address the third group in his audience,
the younger generation to which he himself belongs (541).
The Spartoi he tried to rouse by an appeal to their
proven valour in battle (534 f.; cf. 116 - 26), the
Tyrians by an appeal to their patriotism (439). Now
he plays on the pride in their origins and reputation
of the young men of Thebes (543 ff.). Surely they will
emulate their dragon-grandfather and fight for their
honour against the invader - in this case a bunch of
cissies (547, 555 f.)?

541 *o*: see on 579 below. * *meae*: sc. *aetati*; but the meaning of *aetas* shifts from 540 ('age-group') to 541
('age').

542 *thyrsos*: the *thyrsus* (θύρσος) was a staff, made of a
plant stem wreathed in ivy and vine leaves, often with
a pine cone on top, which the worshippers of Bacchus
shook; cf. Euripides, *Bacchae* 80 f. ἀνὰ θύρσον τε
τινάσσων/κισσῷ τε στεφανωθεὶς/Διόνυσον θεραπεύει
('brandishing the thyrsus and garlanded with ivy he
serves Dionysus'), and for a maenad or follower of
Dionysus with thyrsus, see cover illustration.
* *fronde*: i.e. ivy (cf. the preceding quotation from
Euripides), which was sacred to Bacchus because it
had saved his life as a baby, when the nymphs of Nysa
put a screen of it over his cradle to hide him from
Juno (*Fasti* 3.767 - 70). * *decebat*: Pentheus' choice
of the imperf. tense amounts to a calculated insult.
tenere and *tegi* are the subjects of *decebat*.

543 *qua stirpe*: abl. of origin.

544 *illius*: the quantity of the medial vowel varies according to metrical needs; similarly with the gen. of *iste,
ipse, unus, ullus, nullus, totus*. The gen. of *alius*
is always *alius*, that of *alter* always *alterius* (except
in Ennius).

545 *pro*: 'for', i.e. 'in defence of'.

546 *interiit*: Ovid admits the obsolete quantity of the third
pers. s. ending in the perf., usually in compounds of
eo (*abiit, adiit, periit, subiit, praeteriit* often; *rediit* twice); *petiit* is also frequent, *impediit* occurs
once; cf. 6.658 *prosiluit* and *Her.* 9.141 (possibly not
by Ovid) *occubuit*. * *at*: simply heightens the opposition

of *vos* to *ille*; it need not be translated (cf. 547,
asyndeton). The figure of antithesis is rather over-
worked in this part of the speech.

547 *molles*: applied to men, the adj. = 'effeminate', with
more than a hint of physical loss of virility in this
context.

548 *patrium retinete decus*: 'uphold the fair name of the
fatherland'. * *vetabant*: the imperf. has the sense
of 'were for forbidding' or 'were going to forbid'
(= *vetituri erant*). Instead of a formal apodosis
Ovid substitutes a wish for the present (*utinam diruerent ... sonarent*). Were the sentence to be re-
written as a regular condition, it would have the
form *si vetarent* (→ *vetituri erant* → *vetabant*), *diruerent*, for it has to be unreal, present time. The
fut. part. + a past tense of *esse*, however, expresses
of itself a potential idea, which makes it unnecessary
to use the subjunctive to indicate this. (The same
applies to modal verbs such as *possum* and *debeo*, and
to the gerund or gerundive + a past tense of *esse*.)
But the retention of the indic. is normally seen in
the apodosis (GL 597.2). For the thought and language
in 549, cf. Aen. 8.398 f. '*nec pater omnipotens Troiam
nec fata vetabant/stare*'.

550 *ferrum ignisque sonarent*: *ferrum* stands collectively for
swords, *ignis* for the fires started by the enemy within
the breached walls; cf. Aen. 2.310 ff. '*iam Deiphobi
dedit ampla ruinam/Volçano superante domus, iam proximus ardet/Vcalegon; Sigea igni freta lata relucent*'
and Aen. 2.705 f. '*iam per moenia clarior ignis/audi-
tur, propiusque aestus incendia volvunt*'. For the
same combination in quite a different context, see
698.

551 - 552 *essemus, foret, carerent*: 'we should (in those im-
agined circumstances) be wretched ... ' - an incomplete
unreal condition (pres. time), the protasis of which
has to be supplied from the preceding wish, i.e. *si
tormenta virique moenia diruerent* ... (GL 600). *sors
... foret* and *lacrimae ... carerent* form successive
variations on '*essemus miseri sine crimine*': there
would be no shame (*sine crimine - sors non celanda -
pudore carere*) in going down fighting, though much
suffering (*miseri - sors querenda - lacrimae*).

551 *sine crimine*: 'without reproach', i.e. 'but blameless',
adj. (= *criminis expertes, insontes*).

553 *at nunc*: 'but as things are', 'in reality'. * *puero*:

'boy', a contemptuous older person's term (as in English) for a young man in his late 'teens or even early twenties (cf. 607, 655). Pentheus is perhaps approaching thirty.

554 *quem ... equorum*: expands *inermi*. Bacchus is described by Euripides, *Bacchae* 416 ff., as 'rejoicing in festivities and loving Peace, the goddess who brings prosperity and is the nurse of children'. If he carries no weapons, however, it is also because his powers and the frenzy of his worshippers are more than a match for any army (cf. *Bacchae* 761 ff., 798 ff.).

555 *murra*: a scented ointment made with the gum of the myrrhtree (genus *Commiphora*) of Arabia. With Pentheus' scornful jibe, cf. Turnus' prayer for vengeance against the *semivir Phryx* or 'Phrygian pansy' (i.e. Aeneas): *Aen.* 12.99 f. '*(da) foedare in pulvere crinis/vibratos calido ferro murraque madentis*'. It was from Phrygia and Lydia that Dionysus historically came, a part of the world from which many (in western eyes) unmanly practices were allegedly exported, such as the use of hair oil. In myth the marked oriental character of his cult is explained by his travels through Asia (Euripides, *Bacchae* 13 - 19, Apollodorus 3.5.1 - 2; and Rose (1958) 155 f.). * *crinis*: collective s., as at Horace, *Odes* 1.32.12 f. '*Lycum nigris oculis nigroque/ crine decorum*'.

556 *purpura et pictis intextum vestibus aurum*: further evidence of effeminacy and decadence. *purpura* = 'purple cloth'. *pictis* is proleptic (see on *vitiatas* 76 above), i.e. it is the weaving in of gold thread that makes the garments *pictae* ('brightly decorated'). The Phrygians were famous as embroiderers in gold, lending their name to the profession (*phrygio, -onis*).

557 *quem quidem ego actutum*: both the elisions and the choice of *actutum* (adv.) command attention. Nowhere else does Ovid construct an initial dactyl of three words which before elision amount to five syllables. The scansion smacks not of epic, but of dramatic poetry. It is significant too that *actutum* belongs to the language of tragedy rather than of epic (once only in Virgil: *Aen.* 9.255 f. '*tum cetera reddet/actutum pius Aeneas*'). It would appear that Ovid wished to indicate a debt to an earlier, tragic treatment of the Pentheus story in Latin, namely that of Pacuvius. The clues seem faint, but are of the kind to have attracted the notice of a Roman reader versed in the major genres of his native literature (see Kenney (1973) 120). * *modo absistite*: 'do you but stand aside', parataxis in parenthesis

instead of a subordinate clause of proviso (*dummodo
absistatis*, 'provided that you/if you will only stand
aside').

558 *assumptum*: 'fraudulently claimed' (= *falso arrogatum*).
Both *assumptum* and *commenta* are predicative (supply
esse).

559 *an*: for *an* introducing a single direct question (here
expressive of self-remonstrance), see GL 457, K 405
note 2.   * *Acrisio*: dat. of possessor. Acrisius, the
father of Danaë, was king of Argos. Ovid alone records
his antagonism to Bacchus, of which he eventually re-
pented (4.607), but not before his nieces - or, in
another version, the women of Argos - had been driven
insane by the god. Pentheus did not live long enough
to learn of Acrisius' change of heart; he admires him
for not knuckling under (Apollodorus 2.2.2 (cf. 3.5.2);
and Rose (1958) 153).

560 *venienti*: dat. of (dis)advantage, 'in his face'.

561 *Penthea ... Thebis?*: adversative parataxis with asyndeton,
in lieu of either *Penthea a u t e m ...* or *cum Penthea terreat* ('whereas', 'while'). * *cum totis Thebis*:
'and the whole of Thebes'; for *cum* used in this way,
see on 211 above.

562 *citi*: adj. for adv., a common idiom where ideas of speed
or time are involved; cf. *Aen.* 4.149 f. '*haud illo seg-
nior ibat/Aeneas*', Horace, *Ars Poetica* 269 '*(exemplaria)
nocturna versate manu, versate diurna*'. * *ducem*: i.e.
Bacchus (whom Pentheus does not admit to be divine).

563 *iussis*: 'my orders', n. pl. subst. *mora segnis* is pleonastic; the adj. has an act. force ('that causes slowness').

564 *avus*: Cadmus. * *Athamas*: husband of Ino. * *suorum*:
Pentheus' relatives and dependants.

565 *inhibere laborant*: 'try hard to restrain'. *laboro* + prolative infin. is poetic (first found in Lucilius).

566 *admonitu*: causal abl. * *irritatur*: cf. *Rem. Am.* 133
'*quin etiam accendas vitia irritesque vetando*' (after
Am. 3.4.11).

567 *moderamina ipsa*: 'their very efforts to hold him back'.
The word *moderamen* was coined by Ovid as a metrically
usable synonym of *moderatio* (cf. Cicero, *De Oratore*
2.35 '*languentis populi incitatio et effrenati moder-*

atio'). He uses it seven times in all; see on *tempt-amina* 341 above. * *nocebant*: the switch of tense from artificial, vivid historic pres. (*est, irritatur, crescit*; earlier *corripiunt, laborant*) to true historic imperf. at the end of the sentence has a summarising function, as well as affording a transition back to the historic narrative that is used for the rest of the paragraph.

568 - 569 *sic ego ... vidi*: a highly un-epic intrusion by the poet into his story. This autoptic formula is a transplant from elegy, where illustrations from life, seen or otherwise experienced by the author, are frequently introduced in order to prove a point he is making. The technique features prominently in Ovid's two mock-didactic elegiac works (*Ars Am., Rem. Am.*), which belong to the years immediately preceding the *Metamorphoses*.

568. *eunti*: 'its course'.

569 *modico strepitu*: abl. of manner, grammatically parallel to the adv. *lenius*; see on *placido tenore* 113 above.

570 *quacumque*: balancing, but showing a typical slight variation on, *qua* in 568. * *tenebant*: for *retinebant* (sc. *eum*); cf. 364.

571 *ab obice*: 'as a result of / thanks to the barrier'; see on *ab ictu* 183 above.

572 *cruentati*: Bacchus' followers evidently had put up a stout resistance (cf. 554). * *Bacchus ubi esset*: indir. question dependent on *quaerenti*.

574 *famulum sacrorum*: i.e. a priest of a lowly kind.

575 *post terga*: 'behind his back', a metrically necessary but also logically defensible pl. ('each side of his back'); cf. 74 *rictus*.

576 *quendam secutum*: subst., 'someone who followed', 'some follower of' (= *comitem famulumque* above). [The variant reading *quondam* has its supporters, but a pron. is needed more urgently than an adv. to define the role of the past part.] * *Tyrrhena gente*: abl. of origin, 'Etruscan', i.e. 'Lydian' (cf. 583 *Maeonia*). The adj. neatly 'cues in' the tale of the pirates.

577 *tremendos*: 'terrible'; cf. *Georg.* 4.469 '(*Orpheus*) *Man-isque adiit regemque tremendum*', Horace, *Odes* 4.2.15 f. '*cedidit tremendae/flamma Chimaerae*'.

578 *poenae vix tempora differt*: death by stoning was to be
the punishment of the 'girl-faced stranger' when
caught, according to Euripides' Pentheus (*Bacchae*
356 f.). In Pacuvius, Pentheus puts Acoetes in gaol
as a temporary measure (see on 582 below).

579 *o periture ... dature ...* : such elaborately periphrastic forms of address are restricted to verse; verbal
forms are particularly favoured; cf. Horace, *Epistles*
1.1.1 *'prima dicte mihi, summa dicende Camena'*. The
addition of the interjection *o* to a vocative indicates
powerful emotion; unlike Greek ὦ it is never used in
ordinary address (cf. 713). * *documenta*: pl. for s.,
metri gratia.

580 - 581 *ede tuum nomen nomenque parentum et patriam*: this
corresponds to the question put by Pentheus at *Bacchae*
460 πρῶτον μὲν οὖν μοι λέξον ὅστις εἶ γένος; ('Tell me
first what nationality you are'). Ovid has expanded
it by rendering - quite closely - a Homeric interrog.
formula used for establishing the identity of a stranger; e.g. *Odyssey* 1.170 τίς πόθεν εἰς ἀνδρῶν, πόθι τοι
πόλις ἠδὲ τοκῆες; ('What man are you and from where?
Where is your city and your parents?'). * *morisque
novi cur sacra frequentes*: corresponds (more loosely)
to *Bacchae* 465 πόθεν δὲ τελετὰς τάσδ' ἄγεις ἐς Ἑλλάδα;
('why (not 'whence') do you bring these rites to Greece?').
Note the change of construction from nouns to a noun
clause (indir. question) as objects of *ede*.

581 *moris*: 'way of worshipping', 'cult'.

Acoetes' tale: Bacchus and the Sailors, 582 - 691

582 *metu*: abl. of separation (GL 390.3, K 229 (b), W 41.8).
* *Acoetes*: the figure of Acoetes has no place in Euripides (nor has the episode of the Tyrrhenian Sailors).
He did, however, feature in Pacuvius' play, from which
no fragments remain but of which Servius (note on *Aen.*
4.469) gives a synopsis: '(*Pentheus*) *misit satellites,
qui eum* (i.e. Bacchus) *vinctum ad se perducerent. qui
cum ipsum non invenissent, unum ex comitibus eius Acoe-
ten captum ad Pentheum perduxerunt. is, cum de eo
graviorem poenam constitueret, iussit eum interim
claudi vinctum; cumque sponte sua et carceris fores
apertae essent et vincula Acoeti excidissent, miratus
Pentheus ... Cithaerona petit'*, etc. Unless Ovid found
a precedent in some lost Hellenistic work, it is his
own invention to make Acoetes the narrator of the *Sailors*

tale. Bacchus' abduction by Lydian (Τυρσηνοί) pirates
forms the subject of the seventh Homeric Hymn (cf.
Apollodorus 3.5.3, Hyginus, *Fabulae* 134, *Poetica Astro-
nomica* 2.17; and Rose (1958) 155). Some believe that
Acoetes must be Bacchus himself in disguise. This
would certainly invest the scene with fine dramatic
irony (cf. especially 573 - 4 *'Bacchum vidisse negarunt./"hunc" dixere "tamen ... "*, 658 - 9 (Acoetes is
speaking) *'"nec enim praesentior illo/est deus"'*) and
it would, of course, bring Ovid's account into line
with that of Euripides, in which the god, incognito,
is brought in chains before Pentheus and later over-
throws the walls of the prison to which Pentheus has
committed him (*Bacchae* 432 ff., 509 ff., 585 ff.).
However, Ovid never gives even the slightest hint that
Acoetes is other than an ex-sailor and devotee of Bacchus: he remains *'Tyrrhenus Acoetes'* to the very end
(696). Ovid was clearly content to follow the alternative, Pacuvian tradition concerning the god's first
demonstration of his power to the Theban unbeliever.

583 *patria Maeonia est*: Maeonia was a district of the king-
dom of Lydia in western Asia Minor; cf. Euripides,
Bacchae 464 Λυδία δέ μοι πατρίς ('Lydia is my home-
land'). * *humili de plebe*: origin (partitive).

584 The line exhibits a twofold hyperbaton or transposition
(the Romans' own term was *transgressio*): first, the
subject of the principal clause, *pater*, has been in-
serted into the subordinate (relative) clause; secondly,
the relative clause has absorbed its antecedent, *arva*
(cf. 183, 303).

585 *lanigeros greges*: cf. *Georg.* 3.287 *'lanigeros agitare
greges hirtasque capellas'*. The epithet goes back
to Accius (*praetext.* 20 *'pecus lanigerum eximia pul-
chritudine'*), from whom Lucretius took it (*De Rerum
Natura* 2.318, 2.662, 5.866, 6.1237), whence in turn
Virgil. * *armenta*: 'cattle'. The word can denote
horses or other large animals, but is usually (always,
when opposed to *grex*) restricted to bulls, cows, or
ploughing oxen (just as *grex* commonly denotes sheep,
though it means basically 'herd / drove' of any animal).

586 *et ipse*: 'he too', 'like me'.

586 - 587 *lino, hamis, calamo*: only one method of catching
fish is indicated, namely angling. For *linum = linea*,
'fishing line', cf. 13.923 *'nunc in mole sedens moder-
abar arundine linum'*. Elsewhere *linum* may = *funis* or
sagena, a cast-net (e.g. *Georg.* 1.142). Besides net-
ting and angling, professional fishermen made use of

the fish spear (*iaculum*) and the trap (*nassa*).

588 *ars illi sua census erat*: 'his skill was his wealth'.
For *census* (lit.'rateable value'), cf. Horace, *Odes*
2.15.13 '*privatus illis census erat brevis*'. *sua*
refers to the 'logical', not the grammatical, subject
of the sentence, as often (GL 309.2, K 317 note 2).
* *traderet*: 'was teaching (me)'.

589 *studii*: synonymous with *artis*.

590 *moriens*: 'at his death' (= *mortuus*). The pres. part.
is occasionally employed loosely instead of a past
part.; cf. 573 *quaerenti domino negarunt* (see W 102).

591 *aquas*: either 'water' generally, or more specifically
'his stretch of water' or 'beat'.

592 *ne scopulis haererem semper in isdem*: 'so as not to be
stuck forever on the same old rocks', meant both literally and with a pun on the metaphorical sense of
scopulus, 'difficulty/evil'; cf. Cicero, *Pro Rabirio*
25 '*nec tuas umquam ratis ad eos scopulos appulisses
ad quos Sex. Titi adflictam navem et in quibus C.
Deciani naufragium fortunarum videres*'.

593 - 594 *regimen carinae flectere*: 'to steer a boat', 'be
a helmsman' (*regimen* = *gubernaculum*).

594 *Ōlĕnĭae sidus pluviale Capellae*: an enclosing appositional
structure, the gen. being in apposition to (or defining)
sidus pluviale. Capella is a star in the constellation
Auriga whose heliacal rising coincides with the start
of the Mediterranean rainy season in October. This
Goat Star (also called Capra) was supposedly none other
than Amalthea (see on 2 above) translated to heaven
after her death. The learned epithet commemorates her
supposed birthplace, Olenus in Aetolia, although in
fact this is due to a misunderstanding of the Greek
adj. ὠλένιος ('of' or 'at the elbow', i.e. of the Char-
ioteer) with which the Alexandrian poet Aratus, *Phaeno-
mena* 164, had 'fixed' the star. Yet Cicero got it
right in his translation of Aratus, which Ovid certainly
knew.

595 *Tăÿgĕtēn*: one of the Pleiades; cf. *Georg.* 4.232 '*Taygete
simul os terris ostendit honestum*'. * *Hyadas*; 'the
Rainers', a group of five stars in Taurus, whose rising
and setting delimited the rainy season. In life they
had been the nurses of Dionysus. * *Arcton*: the Great
Bear (cf. 45). * *notavi*: 'marked', 'observed' (*oculis*,
instrumental abl., need hardly be translated), so 'fam-

iliarised myself with'; i.e. he taught himself how to
navigate by the stars. In the next line he claims a
knowledge of meteorology; the two go together as essential skills for a master mariner. 594 and 595 am-
plify the statement *regimen carinae flectere addidici*.

597 *forte*: introducing a story; see on 318 above. * *Chiae
  telluris*: a grandiose circumlocution for *Chii (insulae)*.
  Chios lies off the coast of Lydia.

598 *applicor*: middle (like *adducor* and *immittor* below), 'I
  steer for', 'put in to'; also + dat. in verse. In
  prose *navem applico (ad)* is preferred. * *dextris
  remis*: either 'with skilled/favourable rowing' or
  'turning to port' (using only the oars on the starboard side of the vessel). The latter interpretation
  may seem too technical and precise (requiring Ovid
  to have been quite clear in his own mind that Acoetes
  set sail from northern, not southern, Lydia, i.e. from
  the region of the Gulf of Smyrna, so as to pass to the
  W of Chios). 'Skilled' will imply that the landfall
  was potentially hazardous, 'favourable' that the crew
  experienced no difficulty. * *adducor litora*: for
  the acc. without prep. after a verb of motion, see on
  462 above. With verbs compounded with *ad* the construction appears more natural than with simple *venio* or *eo*
  (e.g. *Aen.* 1.2 f. '*Italiam ... Laviniaque venit/litora*').

599 *do levis saltus*: *do* + noun frequently (in poetry) forms
  a periphrasis for the verb to which the noun is related.
  Here we might substitute *leviter salio*, though something
  will be lost, just as in English 'I leaped' is less
  colourful than 'I gave a leap'. This phrase is Virgilian (*Aen.* 12.681). Similarly e.g. *lacrimas, motum, mug-
  itus, insidias do* = *lacrimo, moveo* (or *moveor*), *mugio,
  insidior*. The pl. *saltus* is *metri causa*, for Acoetes
  jumps down from ship to sand in a single movement (*immittor* + dat. = 'I land on').

600 - 601 *Aurora ... , exsurgo*: parataxis, for *cum primum Aurora ... coepit, exsurgo*. It gives Acoetes' recital a
  simple, matter-of-fact tone (cf. the flatly prosaic
  statement '*nox ibi consumpta est*').

601 - 602 *inferre admoneo*: a poetic construction; see on *perquirere* 3 above.

602 *undas*: not the sea, but a spring (601 *latices recentis*).

603 *ipse*: 'I myself', in opposition to *alios* understood with
  admoneo. * *quid aura mihi promittat*: 'what the wind

holds out for me', i.e. if it is blowing in the right
direction for continuing the voyage to Delos.
* *tumulo ab alto*: with *prospicio*, not *promittat*.
The hyperbaton makes it impossible to mark off the
dependent indir. question with a comma (cf. 634 - 5).

605 *adsumus en*: 'Here we are, see'. * *Opheltes*: Ovid names
eleven sailors (there were twenty all told: 687), the
author of the seventh Homeric Hymn none. The other
writer to give names is Hyginus (*Fabulae* 134, *Tyrrheni*),
who promises twelve (including Acoetes) but supplies
only eleven. Ovid and Hyginus agree on the following:
Opheltes, Medon, Lycabas, Libys, Dictys, Alcimedon and
Epopeus; Hyginus' Melas and Aethalides are plainly the
same as Ovid's Melanthus and Aethalion. Simon is ex-
clusive to Hyginus, Proreus to Ovid. H. J. Rose, in
his edition of Hyginus (Leiden, 1939), argues that he
was not indebted to Ovid (Introduction viii ff.).
Both then will have consulted a common, lost Hellenistic source.

606 *utque putat*: the clause should logically follow *praedam*;
i.e. *praedamque, ut putat, nactus,* 'having come across
some booty (as he thinks)'.

607 *virginea forma*: abl. of description or quality. In the
Homeric Hymn (73 ff.) Bacchus is 'like a young man in
first adulthood', with long dark locks and purple
cloak - not at all girlish.

608 *mero somnoque gravis*: cf. Livy 29.34.11 'alios·vino et
somno gravis (acc. pl.) arma capere'.

609 *vix*: = *aegre* (cf. 71). * *cultum faciemque gradumque*:
'his attire, his features and the way he walked'.

610 *ibi*: i.e. *in* or *ex illis* (*rebus*).

611 - 612 *quod numen in isto corpore sit, dubito*: 'I am not
sure what divinity is in that body'. The following
affirmation ('*sed corpore numen in isto est*') reverses
the order of the two nouns (chiasmus).

613 *quisquis es*: a typical 'blanket' formula of address in
hymns or prayers, where the preferred title of the
god or goddess is uncertain; cf Aeschylus, *Agamemnon*
160 ff. Ζεὺς ὅστις πότ᾽ ἐστιν, εἰ τόδ᾽ αὐ-/τῷ φίλον
κεκλημένῳ,/τοῦτο νιν προσεννέπω ('Zeus, whosoever he
is, if that style please him, if that do I address
him'), Catullus 34.21 f. (to Diana) '*sis quocumque
tibi placet/sancta nomine*', *Aen*. 4.576 f. '*sequimur
te, sancte deorum,/quisquis es*'. * *faveas ... adsis*:

'look favourably upon (or 'befriend') us and help our
labours'.

614 *mitte precari*: 'cease / give up praying'. The construction with prolative infin. is found in classical prose
as well as in verse; similarly *omitto* + infin.

615 - 616 *quo non alius ... rudente relabi*: a parody of Virgil's description of Misenus: *Aen.* 6.164 f. *'quo non
praestantior alter/aere ciere viros Martemque accendere
cantu'*. * *conscendere, relabi*: epexegetic (explana-
tory) infins. with *ocior* (GL 421 note 1.c, K 373, W 26),
'swifter at climbing up ... and sliding back down'.

616 *prenso rudente*: abl. absolute, virtually instrumental.

617 - 620 *hoc ... hoc ... hoc ... hoc*: threefold anaphora
with asyndeton, perhaps intended to suggest the repeated shouts of agreement from the others.

617 *flavus, prorae tutela, Melanthus*: for the order see on
420 above. The *prorae tutela* is the forward lookout
(cf. 634). Ovid lightheartedly gives yellow hair
(*flavus*) to Melanthus, whose name lit. means 'Black-
bloom' (cf. Hyginus' Melas, 'Black'), though this
possibly denotes skin colour ('swarthy').

618 - 619 *qui ... remis*: Epopeus gives the timing of the
stroke to the oarsmen (*remis = remigibus* by metonymy);
hortator is the proper technical term (= κελευστής).
He did not, as the Penguin translator has it, 'appor-
tion spells of rest'. The organisation of watches
would be Acoetes' responsibility.

620 *praedae tam caeca cupido est*: a moralising epigram,
akin to Virgil, *Aen.* 3.56 f. *'quid non mortalia pectora cogis,/auri sacra fames?'*. For *praedae cupido*,
see 225.

621 *tamen*: 'no matter what you say'. * *sacro pondere*: for
pondere sacri hominis (= *dei*). * *pinum*: a common
poetic metonymy for *navis* (material instead of manufactured object), just as *carina* (607, 614) is a standard synecdoche for the same (part for whole).

622 *perpetiar*: for the simple verb *patiar* (cf. 8 *requirit*).
* *pars hic mihi maxima iuris*: 'mine is the highest
authority here', i.e. 'I'm the captain of this ship!'
iuris is partitive gen.

623 *aditu*: 'the gangplank'. * *furit*: 'flies into a rage'.

624 *Tusca*: 'Lydian'. The ancients believed - perhaps correctly - that the Etruscans (*Tusci*, *Tyrrheni*) had mig-
rated to Italy from Lydia; see Herodotus 1.94.5 ff.

625 *exilium, poenam*: in apposition; cf. 4 - 5.

626 *resto*: 'I stand my ground' (= *resisto*); cf. 623 *obsisto*.

626 - 627 *guttura pugno rupit*: 'dealt me a crushing blow to
the throat with his fist'.

627 *excussum*: past. part. (sc. *me*); cf. *Aen*. 1.115 f. '*ex-
cutitur (de nave) pronusque magister/volvitur in caput*'.
* *si non*: for *nisi*; see on 4 above and cf. 271.

628 *amens*: 'semi-conscious', 'stunned'.

630 *Bacchus enim fuerat*: 'for it had been Bacchus all along'.
* *veluti*: introduces a conditional or 'unreal' comparative clause with the subj. (GL 602, K 449.ii, W
254). *velut si, quasi* or *tamquam si* would be preferred
in prose.

631 *aque mero*: for the position of *-que*, cf. *Georg*. 4.347
'*aque Chao*'. Enclitic particles like *-que, -ne* and
-ve are (in prose) not normally attached to a mono-
syllabic prep. but to the dependent noun or adj.

632 - 633 *quid ... quis ... qua ... quo*: each of the four
questions is introduced by a different case or gender
of the interrog. pron. (the last, *quo*, is adv.). For
a similar artistic *variatio*, cf. 442 and 444, 654.
* *qua ope*: 'by what means?' (lit. 'help'), 'how?'.

634 *Proreus*: by virtue of his name (πρωρεύς, 'bow-man', i.e.
forward lookout) he should have had Melanthus' job
(617).

635 *ede*: 'say', governing the indir. question *quos portus
contingere velis*, into which it has been incorporated
(cf. 603 - 4). * *terra sistere petita*: 'you will be
put ashore in the country you want', local abl., the
past part. having a purely adj. force ('requested',
'desired').

636 *Naxon*: no prep. is required as Naxos is a (small) island
(GL 337, K 271). For the Greek acc. ending, cf. 595,
597 (GL 65, K 68).

637 *domus*: Naxos (or Dia: see 690) was an ancient centre of
Bacchic worship; cf. *Aen*. 3.125 '*bacchatamque iugis
Naxon*'. According to the first Homeric Hymn, Naxos

was one of the many places that claimed to be Bacchus'
birthplace. It was on Naxos that the Cretan princess
Ariadne, abandoned by her lover Theseus, was found and
wedded by Bacchus (Catullus 64.251 ff., Apollodorus,
Epitome 1.9; and Rose (1958) 265 f.). Ovid makes him
sound like a hospitable Roman, inviting the crew to
come in for refreshments before going on their way.

638 *fallaces*: predicative, 'the liars'.

639 *pictae*: a standing epithet of ships, which were (and
still are in the Mediterranean) painted with bands of
colour and often a pair of eyes. Homeric ships, however, are 'black' or 'dark-coloured' through being
covered in pitch (e.g. Homer, *Iliad* 1.300).

640 *dextrā*: adv., 'on the right', 'to starboard'. [The variant reading *dextera* makes good sense, but the repetition with change of ictus *déxtra ... dextrá* is more
in keeping with Ovid's and other poets' practice.]
* *dextra lintea danti*: 'as I set the sail to steer
to starboard' (not 'with my right hand'). For *lintea* =
vela, cf. *Aen*. 3.686, Horace, *Odes* 1.14.9.

642 *pro se quisque*: 'each man (cries) on his own behalf',
'of his own accord'. [But the text here is irremed-
iably corrupt; see Introduction p. 14.] * *laevam
pete*: cf. *Aen*. 3.563 '*laevam cuncta cohors remis ven-
tisque petivit*' (understand *partem*).

643 *aure*: 'in my ear', simple abl. for *in aure*.

644 *moderamina*: here = *gubernaculum*; see on 567 and 341 above.

645 *ministerio scelerisque artisque*: lit. 'from the perform-
ance of a crime and my skill' (as helmsman). Acoetes
will not use his skill to further a crime.

646 Theme ('*increpor a cunctis*') and variation ('*totumque
immurmurat agmen*', sc. *mihi*).

647 *scilicet*: ironic, as the speaker's action shows (648 - 9).

648 *subit*: 'comes and takes my place'. * *petit diversa*:
'steers in the opposite direction' (*loca* is to be understood with *diversa*).

650 *tamquam*: with subj. (*senserit*), for *tamquam si* (cf. 630).

653 *terra rogata*: see on *terra petita* 635 above.

655 *puerum iuvenes, multi unum*: the antitheses are arranged

chiastically (ABBA).

656 *flebam*: for the tense, see GL 234, K 105 (a) note 1.

658 *per tibi nunc ipsum*: sc. *deum*; 'I swear to you now by
 the god himself'. The separation of *per* from its case
 in oaths is common; e.g. *per ego te deos oro, per ego
 vobis deos atque homines dico*. *adiuro* = *iuro*, compound
 for simple verb.

659 - 660 *tam ... fide*: 'that I am telling you the truth,
 though it outstrips credibility' (lit. 'belief in the
 truth'). *veri* is objective gen. The correlatives
 tam ... quam are used much like *ut ... sic (ita)* with
 concessive force; see on 188 - 9 above.

660 *stetit*: see on 20 above.

661 *quam si siccum navale teneret*: 'than if it were resting
 in dry dock'. For this sense of *teneo*, cf. 2. *puppis*
 (= *navis*) remains the subject.

662 *remorum in verbere perstant*: 'they keep on flailing the
 oars'. *remorum* is either a possessive (subjective)
 gen., *verbere* being the beating done by the oars on
 the water, or an objective gen.; cf. Lucan 3.535 - 6
 '*praetoria puppis/verberibus sēnis agitur*' ('by the
 strokes of six oars a side').

663 *deducunt*: 'unfurl', 'let down' (from the yardarm). *vela*
 = 'sail' not 'sails', for ships of the period had only
 the one, square-rigged; the pl. is much commoner than
 the s. in both prose and verse. * *gemina ope*: cf.
 Aen. 3.563 (quoted on 642 above), and the proverbial
 remis velis(que), 'with all speed', 'with might and
 main'.

665 *distingunt*: 'adorn'.

666 *ipse*: Bacchus. * *racemiferis frontem circumdatus uvis*:
 'his brow wreathed with clustering grapes'. For the
 construction, see on 162 above.

668 *quem circa*: like other dissyllabic preps. *circa* often
 follows its case, though in Cicero this is restricted
 to where the word governed is a pron. (GL 413).
 * *tigres simulacraque inania lyncum*: i.e. *simulacra
 inania tigrum et lyncum*. These animals, with the leopard (669; also necessarily *simulacra*), were sacred
 to Bacchus, the tiger especially; cf. Virg. *Ecl*. 5.29
 f. '*Daphnis et Armenias curru subiungere tigris/instit-
 uit, Daphnis thiasos inducere Bacchi*'. For lynxes, cf.

Propertius 3.17.6 (to Bacchus) *'lyncibus ad caelum
vecta Ariadna tuis'*. The maenad or follower of Bacchus in the cover illustration not only carries a
leopard but also wears a leopard skin over her shoulder.

669 *pictarum*: 'multi-coloured', i.e. 'spotted', which the
panther (black leopard) is not. * *pantherarum*: spondaic quadrisyllables at the end of the verse, giving
a spondaic fifth foot, are usually confined to Greek
proper names or Greek loan words (as here); but pure
Latin words of this shape, other than proper names,
occur sporadically in Ovid, e.g. 5.165 *armentorum*,
6.69 *argumentum*.

670 *exiluere*: 'leaped to their feet' (they were rowing),
not 'leaped overboard', for which Ovid uses *desilire*
(cf. 681 below).

670 - 671 *sive ... timor*: 'smitten either by madness or by
terror'. For *sive ... sive* of alternative explanations,
see on 46 - 7 above.

672 *corpore*: abl. of respect. * *expresso spinae curvamine*:
'with sharply curving back', abl. of manner modifying
flecti. *expressus* = 'prominent' (lit. 'forced up',
'raised').

673 - 674 *in quae miracula verteris?*: 'what sort of monster
are you turning into?'; cf. *Georg.* 4.441 (of Proteus)
'omnia transformat sese in miracula rerum'.

674 *loquenti*: dat. of reference; see on *loquenti* 357 above.

675 *naris*: nom.; here = 'nose', as in the phrases *emunctae*
and *obesae naris*. * *erat*: more or less = *fiebat*, parallel to *trahebat*, inceptive imperf. * *squamam, durata*: dolphins, unlike fish, have soft skins without
scales. Ovid, however, had no first-hand acquaintance
with the animal.

676 *at*: not adversative, but indicating a switch to another
grammatical subject; cf. 1.283 f. *'ipse tridente suo
terram percussit. at illa/intremuit'* ('it in turn ... ').
* *obstantis dum vult obvertere remos*: 'in the course
of trying to ship (or 'park') the jammed oars'. For
this nautical sense of *obvertere* (= μεταστρέφειν) cf.
11.475 (part of a detailed description of operations
on board ship) *'obvertit lateri pendentes navita remos'*,
i.e. he lifts the blades of the 'dangling' oars clear
of the water and slides the handles inboard, so that
they rest on the gunwale, *sloping up at an angle*. The

next step would be to free them from the thole-pins
and stow them under the thwarts (cf. 11.486 *remos sub-
ducere*). The oars resist Libys' efforts because they
are entangled in ivy (664).

677 - 678 The acc. and infins. with *vidit* convey the mental
appreciation by the character of what is happening,
not merely his ocular perception of the change. Ovid
gets inside the mind of Libys, whose rapidly changing
definition of his own extremities is subtly brought
out by the asyndetic anaphora *iam (non)* .... *iam* ...
For a similar (but voiced) reaction to metamorphosis,
cf. 4.584 - 5 (Cadmus) '"*me tange, manumque/accipe,
dum manus est, dum non totum occupat anguis*"'.

679 *dare bracchia*: 'to stretch out his arms', so as to un-
ravel the rigging.

680 This time the point of view remains the observer's.
  * *repandus*: poetic shorthand for *rostro repando* (descriptive abl.). The epithet recalls Pacuvius' famous
description of dolphins as '*Nerei repandirostrum in-
curvicervicum pecus*' (fragment 352), which Lucilius
later echoed in his *Satires* (fragment 235): '*lascivire
pecus nasi rostrique repandum*'.

681 *falcata novissima cauda est*: 'the end (or 'trailing edge')
of his tail was curved'.

682 *qualia*: for *qualis* introducing a simile without correlative *talis* or other phrase, cf. *Aen.* 3.677 ff. '*cer-
nimus* .../*Aetnaeos fratres caelo capita alta ferentis,/
concilium horrendum: quales cum vertice celso/aeriae
quercus aut coniferae cupressi/constiterunt*'. The comparison with the horns of the *half* moon implies that
Ovid (correctly) did not visualise a narrowly sickle-
shaped tail (despite the derivation of *falcatus* from
falx), which would rather resemble the shape of the
new moon.

683 *undique dant saltus*: 'everywhere they spring clear', i.e.
the remaining pirates, now transformed, jump into the
sea; *undique* connotes *omnes*. To ascribe the leaping
to dolphins already in the water not only omits an
essential stage in the narrative, namely the fate of
the rest of the crew, but also anticipates and so nul-
lifies the point of the following three verbs, *rorant*,
emergunt and *redeunt*, the last two of which describe
the 'porpoising' of the animals through the waves.
Furthermore, as *saltus do* has already been used of Acoetes leaping from the ship (599), it is likely that
the phrase has the same application here. * *rorant*:

intrans., 'are drenched' or 'enveloped'. The 'cloud
of spray' is caused by the impact of their bodies
falling from the ship.

684 *emerguntque iterum*: 'and re-emerge' (antithetic to *ror-*
ant). * *rursus*: not parallel to *iterum*, but = πάλιν,
'back again', reinforcing the prefix of the verb (*red-*
eo).

685 *in chori speciem*: 'after the fashion of / like an ensemble
of dancers'. * *lasciva*: virtually adv., 'playfully'.

686 *acceptum*: two meanings are present, 'that they have
swallowed' and 'welcome', 'pleasing'. The former applies to them as men, the latter to them as dolphins.
mare = 'seawater'.

687 *de modo viginti*: 'out of twenty a moment ago', *de* (partitive) governing the indecl. numeral. *modo* = *nuper*.

688 - 689 *pavidum ... meo*: 'terrified and trembling, my body
cold and scarcely belonging to me'. *corpore* is abl.
of description.

689 *firmat*: 'fortifies', 'reassures'. * *dicens*: very rarely
indeed in classical Latin is dir. speech introduced
by a pres. part. of a verb of saying. In this it differs from Greek.

690 *Dīam tene*: 'head for Dia (Naxos)'. For this sense of
tenere (= *cursum tenere ad*), cf. Livy 36.21.1 '*Anti-*
ochus ... a Chalcide profectus Tenum primo tenuit'.
* *delatus*: 'carried' (sc. *vento*).

691 *accessi sacris*: 'I joined in the rites', after which
Acoetes became a regular participant in them (*fre-*
quento), apparently as a kind of priest (cf. 574 *fam-*
ulum sacrorum).

Pentheus (concluded), 692 - 734

692 *longis ambagibus*: 'your interminable ramblings'. That
the choleric and prejudiced Pentheus should have lis-
tened to Acoetes' tale for more than a minute without
cutting him off is improbable, but Ovid does not aim
at this degree of verisimilitude. He has at least
sought to furnish a motive for Pentheus' unusual for-
bearance (693 '*ut ira mora vires absumere posset*').

695 *Stygiae demittere nocti*: *Stygia nox* stands for Hades'
   realm; cf. the Homeric ῎Αϊδι προϊάπτειν, for which
   Virgil has *Orco demittere* (*Aen.* 2.398, 9.527). The
   dat. of direction is poetic (GL 358, K 227, W 57).

697 *iussae*: see on *iussos* 105 above.

698 *ferrumque ignesque*: 'cold steel and fire' - best taken
   as if in apposition to *instrumenta necis*, though the
   first *-que* appears to connect *ferrum* to *instrumenta*.

699 - 700 Cf. Euripides, *Bacchae* 585 ff., 614 ff., 641 ff.
   The anaphora of *sponte sua* well catches the nature of
   fama, repeated by one person after another. The effect
   of the figure is redoubled by its position at the beginning of consecutive lines, to achieve which in 700
   sponte sua has been postponed from the beginning of
   its clause, a comparative rarity in anaphora (cf. *Rem.*
   Am. 69 f. '*me duce damnosas, homines, compescite curas,/*
   rectaque cum sociis me duce navis eat'). For the
   phrase itself in this context, see Servius' account
   of Pacuvius' *Pentheus* (quoted on 582 above).

701 *nec iubet ire*: sc. *alium quemquam*. With this omitted,
   iubet and *ipse* ('in person') make an elliptical antithesis.

702 *ubi*: for *eo* ('to that place'), *ubi*. * *electus Cithaeron*:
   the choice of Cithaeron is based on considerations of
   topography: it is close to Thebes, and has a level,
   treeless and secluded area on it (708 f.). For Bacchus' association with the mountain, cf. (from an unknown tragedy, possibly Pacuvius' *Antiopa*) '*Liber,*
   qui augusta haec loca Cithaeronis colis' (*trag. incert.*
   fragment 81). * *facienda ad sacra*: gerundive after
   ad to express purpose (GL 432 f., K 379, W 207.4.a and
   151.2).

703 *cantibus, voce*: causal abls.

704 *ut*: introducing a simile, with which cf. *Georg.* 3.83 ff.
   '*(equus) tum, si qua sonum procul arma dedere,/stare*
   loco nescit, micat auribus et tremit artus,/collectum-
   que premens volvit sub naribus ignem'. *acer* = *animosus*,
   fortis. * *aere canoro*: *aes* = *tuba* by metonymy (material for the manufactured object); cf. *Aen.* 9.503 f.
   '*at tuba terribilem sonitum procul aere canoro/increpuit*'.

705 *pugnaeque assumit amorem*: refers to the horse, not the
   tubicen. * *assumit*: lit. 'takes on', so 'is filled with'.

706 The correspondence between the simile and the narrative

is grammatically out of alignment, i.e. *equus* (nom.)
is not answered by *Pentheus* (nom.); instead we have
Penthea (acc.) as the object of the first clause (*ictus ... movit*), while an unexpressed *Pentheo* (possessive, or 'sympathetic', dat.) is to be understood in
the second (*et ... ira*). This lack of balance is due
to Ovid's desire to stress that it is the *sound* that
is the important thing - its quality and its effect.

708 - 709 *monte fere medio est ... campus*: the briefest of
ecphrases, setting ,the scene for the last act of the
drama. It is marked off by the adv. *hic* (710).

708 *cingentibus ultima silvis*: 'its edges (extremities) bor-
dered by woods'.

709 *purus ab*: cf. e.g. *vacuus ab, liber ab* (GL 390.3 note
1, W 40.8). * *spectabilis*: lit. 'visible' (ὁρατός),
so 'that can be overlooked'.

710 *profanis*: lit. 'in front of, outside the sanctuary',
from *pro* (= *extra*) + *fanum*, so 'uninitiated', 'irrev-
erent'; cf. Horace, *Odes* 3.1.1 '*odi profanum vulgus
et arceo*'.

711 - 713 *prima ... mater*: cf. Euripides, *Bacchae* 1114 πρώτη
δὲ μήτηρ ἦρξεν ἱερία φόνου ('his mother, like a priestess, began the killing') and 1179. The double anaphora
prima ... prima ... prima builds up suspense to the
delayed and so all the more horrific revelation of the
identity of the person - *mater*. Ovid does not specify
that Pentheus was spying on the Bacchanals from a tree,
as in Euripides and [Theocritus] 26. Since Agave mis-
takes him for a boar here (715), not a lion cub (e.g.
Bacchae 1174, 1185), we are probably to think of him
as on the ground, peering out from the encircling woods.

712 *suum*: an affective use, 'her own', i.e. 'whom she herself bore', adding to the pathos of the situation by
emphasising the unnatural action of the mother.
* *violavit*: 'wounded' (= *vulneravit* or *sauciavit*,
both unmetrical).

713 *o*: see on 579 above. [The variant *io* for *et o* is attrac-
tive but lacks authoritative Ms. support; cf. 728.]

714 *maximus*: for the position of the superlative, inside the
relative clause, see GL 616.3, K 332 note 1.

715 *omnis in unum*: a favourite type of number-antithesis;
cf. e.g. 544 '*qui multos perdidit unus*', 655 '*si multi
fallitis unum*'.

716 *cunctae coeunt trepidumque sequuntur*: cf. the description
of the pursuit and capture of Actaeon by his hounds,
especially 227 *sequuntur*, 236 *cetera turba coit*. It
is indeed to Autonoë, Actaeon's mother, that Pentheus
first appeals for mercy, showing that the poet and the
character are aware of the parallel.

717 - 718 The four phrases introduced by *iam* form an emotional
climax, culminating in what was for Pentheus the sup-
reme humiliation, having to confess the error of his
ways (*'se peccasse fatentem'*). The triple anaphora,
aided by the three-fold terminal rhyme of the pres.
part. acc. endings, articulates the successive stages
in his mental disintegration.

720 *animos*: 'your feelings'.

721 *quis Actaeon*: indir. question, verb (*sit*) omitted; see
on *unde* 97 above. All the blind madness of the Bac-
chanal is encapsulated in these four words, *'illa
quis Actaeon nescit'*.

722 *Inoo raptu*: for *raptu Inus*, the adj. replacing a possessive gen.; see on *sanguine erili* 140 above. * *altera*:
'his left arm'. *manus* (here = *bracchium*, 'forearm')
has to be supplied from *dextram* (*manum*) in 721.

723 *non habet bracchia*: again cf. Actaeon's plight, 241
'circumfert tacitos tamquam sua bracchia vultus'. A
closer verbal parallel occurs at 1.635 f. (of Io)
*'Argo cum bracchia vellet/tendere, non habuit quae
bracchia tenderet Argo'*.

724 *sed*: postponed from its proper position for metrical
reasons, as not uncommonly in verse. Very rarely are
conjs. displaced by more than one place. * *trunca
vulnera*: lit. 'dismembered wounds', so 'bleeding
stumps'. His arms below the elbows have gone.

725 *visis*: sc. *quibus* or *his* (*vulneribus*), abl. absolute
with temporal force ('at the sight of them').

726 *collaque ... crinem*: characteristic manifestations of
Bacchic ecstasy; cf. e.g. Euripides, *Bacchae* 695, Catullus 64.255, *Aen.* 7.394.

727 *avulsum caput*: cf. *Georg.* 4.523 *'caput a cervice revul-
sum'* (the head of Orpheus, also torn to pieces by Bacchanals). The reader is spared a description of the
act of wrenching Pentheus' head from his shoulders.
We first see the object after its detachment, which
is dramatically much more effective; cf. Horace, *Satires*

2.3.303 f. *'quid, caput abscisum demens cum portat
Agaue/gnati infelicis, sibi tunc furiosa videtur?'*.

728 *io comites*: cf. Aen. 7.400 *'(Amata) clamat "io matres
audite, ubi quaeque, Latinae"'*. * *victoria nostra*:
in apposition to *opus hoc* - 'this deed of mine spells
victory for us'.

730 *iamque male haerentes*: 'and unable to adhere any longer'.
For *male* in this sense, see on *male sanus* 474 above.
The simile of the autumn leaves is a routine one, its
application distinctly unusual.

731 *manibus nefandis*: for *manibus turbae nefandae*, by a common type of transference of epithet from the whole to
the part most involved in the action.

732 - 733 The book closes with the equivalent of a fable-
writer's 'moral': it is better to worship Bacchus than
deny him. Ovid does not mention the joyous acceptance
of the god by the aged Cadmus and Tiresias, which is
so prominent a feature of Euripides' play. In focus-
sing solely on the womenfolk of Thebes he is preparing
the ground for the opening of Book 4, which tells first
of the fate of Pentheus' female counterparts, the daughters of Minÿas.

733 *tura dant*: 'they make offerings of incense'. * *Ismenides*: see on 169 above.

VOCABULARY

A

ăbeo, -ire, -ii (-ivi), -ĭtum, go away, depart; turn into.

absisto, -ĕre, -stĭti, stand aside, withdraw.

abstrăho, -ĕre, -xi, -ctum, draw, drag away.

absum, -esse, āfui, be away, absent.

absūmo, -ĕre, -mpsi, -mptum, take away; consume.

accēdo, -ĕre, -cessi, -cessum, approach; join (intrans.).

accendo, -ĕre, -di, -sum, set on fire.

accĭpio, -ĕre, -cēpi, -ceptum, receive.

ācer, -cris, -cre, sharp; eager, fierce.

Ăchăĭs -ĭdĭs, f. adj., Achaean, Greek.

ăcies, -ēi, f., edge, point; glance.

actūtūm, adv., immediately.

ăcūmen, -ĭnis, n., point.

ăcūtus, -a, -um, sharp, shrill.

addisco, -ĕre, -dĭdĭci, learn in addition.

addo, -ĕre, -dĭdi, -dĭtum, add, give.

addūco, -ĕre, -duxi, -ductum, draw to; draw up, wrinkle.

ădĕo, -īre, -ĭi, -ĭtum, approach.

adhĭbeo, -ēre, -ui, -ĭtum, apply, employ.

ădhūc, as yet, still.

ădĭmo, -ĕre, -ēmi, -emptum, take away.

ădĭtus, -ūs, m., entrance, approach.

adiūro, -are, -āvi, -ātum, swear (to or by).

admīror, -ari, -atus, wonder (at).

admŏneo, -ēre, -ui, -ĭtum, advise, suggest.

admŏnĭtus, -ūs, m., reminder, reproof.

admŏveo, -ēre, -mōvi, -mōtum, bring to, put to.

ădōro, -are, -āvi, -ātum, worship, pray to.

adsum, -esse, -fui, be present; appear; help.

ăduncus, -a, -um, bent, curved.

advĕna, -ae, m. or f., stranger.

adversus, -a, -um, facing.

adverto, -ĕre, -ti, -sum, turn towards, to.

aequor, -ŏris, n., sea.

aequus, -a, -um, even; favourable; equal.

āēr, ăĕris, m., air.

āēs, āĕris, n., bronze; anything made of bronze e.g. cymbals.

aestus, -ūs, m., heat.

aetas, -ātis, f., age, generation.

aeternus, -a, -um, eternal, lasting.

aethēr, -ĕris, m., air, heaven.

aethĕrĭus, -a, -um, of the heavens, celestial.

aevum, -i, n., age, life-span.

affĕro, -ferre, attŭli, allatum, bring to.

afflātus, -ūs, m., breathing, breath.

afflo, -are, -āvi, -ātum, breathe on.

Ăgēnŏrĕus, -a, -um, of Agenor.

ăger, -ri, m., land, field.

ăgĭto, -are, -āvi, -ātum, drive; be engaged in; brandish.

agmen, -ĭnis, n., band, troop, column.

ăgo, -ĕre, ēgi, actum, drive; do; spend (time); accomplish.

āio, ăis, ăit, say.

albeo, -ēre, be white.

albĭdus, -a, -um, white.

albus, -a, -um, white; album, -i, n., white.

ălĭēnus, -a, -um, foreign, strange, unnatural.

ălĭmentum, -i, n., nourishment, food.

ălĭquis, -qua, -quid, some one.

ălĭter, otherwise.

ălius, -a, -ud, other.

ălo, -ĕre, -ui, -ĭtum, nourish.

alter, -ĕrius, one, other (of two).

alternus, -a, -um, alternate, answering.

altus, -a, -um, high, tall.

alvus, -i, f., womb, belly.

ămans, -ntis, m., lover.

ambāges, -is, *f.* roundabout way; rigmarole.

ambĭguus, -a, -um, doubtful; ambiguum, -i, *n.*, doubt, uncertainty.

āmens, -tis, senseless, distraught.

amīcus, -a, -um, friendly.

amnis, is, *m.*, river.

āmo, -are, -āvi, -ātum, love.

āmor, -ōris, love.

amplector, -i, -plexus, embrace.

anguĭgĕna, -ae, *m.*, born of a serpent *or* dragon.

anguis, -is, *m.*, snake.

anīlis, -e, of an old woman.

anĭma, -ae, *f.*, breath, life, soul.

anĭmus, -i, *m.*, mind; courage, spirit.

annus, -i, *m.*, year.

antĕ, (+ *acc.*), before; *adv.* before, sooner.

antemna, -ae, *f.*, sailyard.

antĭcĭpo, -are, -āvi, -ātum, forestall.

antrum, -i, *n.*, cave, grotto.

ănus, -ūs, *f.*, old woman.

Āŏnĭus, -a, -um, belonging to Aonia, Boeotian.

ăper, -ri, *m.*, wild boar.

appāreo, -ēre, -ui, -ītum, appear, be seen.

appello, -are, -āvi, -ātum, call.

applĭco, -are, -āvi, -ātum, bring near to; bring to land.

aptus, -a, -um, fit, suitable.

ăqua, -ae, *f.*, water.

āra, -ae, *f.*, altar.

ărātrum, -i, *n.*, plough.

arbĭter, -ri, *m.*, judge, umpire.

arbor, -ōris, *f.*, tree.

Arcăs, -ădis, *m.*, Arcadian.

arceo, -ēre, -ui, -ctum, hold off; prevent.

arcus, -ūs, *m.*, bow, arch, vault.

ardeo, -ēre, arsi, burn, blaze.

arduus, -a, -um, high, steep.

argenteus, -a, -um, silvery, of silver.

Argŏlĭcus, -a, -um, of Argos.

arma, -ōrum, *n.pl.*, arms, weapons.

armentum, -i, *n.*, herd.

armĭger, -ĕra, -ĕrum, bearing arms.

armus, -i, *m.*, shoulder.

armo, -are, -āvi, -ātum, arm.

arrideo, -ēre, -risi, -risum, laugh (at *or* with), smile (at *or* upon).

ars, -tis, *f.*, skill, art; craft.

artus, -ūs, *m.*, limb.

arvum, -i, *n.*, field.

aspergo, -ĭnis, *f.*, sprinkling, spray.

aspĭcio, -ēre, -spexi, -spectum, see, look at.

assentio, -ire, (-ior, -iri), give assent to.

assŏno, -are, respond to.

assūmo, -ēre, -mpsi, -mptum, take, gain; claim.

asto, -are, -stĭti, stand up *or* by.

astŭpeo, -ēre, be amazed at.

āter, -ra, -rum, black, dark.

attĕnuo, -are, -āvi, -ātum, make thin, wear away.

attŏnĭtus, -a, -um, thunderstruck, spell-bound.

attŏno, -are, -ui, -ĭtum, thunder at, stupefy.

attrăho, -ēre, -traxi, -tractum, bring, drag to.

auctor, -ōris, *m.*, originator, cause; leader, teacher.

audax, -ācis, bold.

audio, -ire, -ii (-ivi), -ītum, hear.

aufĕro, -ferre, abstŭli, ablātum, carry, take, wrench away.

augur, -ŭris, *m. or f.*, soothsayer, diviner.

augŭror, -ari, -atus, prophesy, foretell.

aulaeum, -i, *n.*, theatre - curtain.

aura, -ae, *f.*, breeze, air (*generally* pl.).

auris, -is, *f.*, ear.

Aurōra, -ae, *f.*, (goddess of) dawn.

aurum, -i, *n.*, gold.

Aūtŏnŏëĭus, -a, -um, of Autonoë.

autumnus, -i, *m.*, autumn.

āvello, -ēre, -velli *or* -vulsi, -vulsum, tear off.

āverto, -ēre, -ti, -sum, turn aside (*trans.*)

āvus, -i, *m.*, grandfather.

B

Bacchēus, -a, -um, } of Bacchus.
Bacchĭcus, -a, -um,
bacchor, -ari, -atus, keep the festival of Bacchus, revel.
băcŭlum, -i, n., staff.
beātus, -a, -um, blessed.
bellĭcus, -a, -um, of war, military.
bellum, -i, n., war.
bĕnĕ, well; quite.
bĭbo, -ĕre, bĭbi, drink.
bĭs, twice.
blandus, -a, -um, fond, caressing.
Boeōtĭus, -a, -um, Boeotian.
bōs, bŏvis, m. or f., bull, cow, ox, heifer.
bracchium, -ii, n., arm.
brĕvis, -e, short.

C

căcūmĭno, -are, -āvi, -ātum, make pointed.
cădo, -ĕre, cĕcĭdi, cāsum, fall.
caecus, -a, -um, blind.
caedes, -is, f., slaughter.
caelum, -i, n., heaven, sky.
caerŭleus, -a, -um, } sea or dark
caerulus, blue.
călămus, -i, m., reed, fishing-rod.
călesco, -ĕre, grow hot, glow.
campus, -i, m. plain.
candĭdus, -a, -um, white, gleaming.
candor, -ōris, m., whiteness, brilliance.
cănis, -is, m. or f., dog, hound.
cănōrus, -a, -um, tuneful, melodious.
cantus, -ūs, m., song.
cānus, -a, -um, white, grey.
cāni, -orum, m. pl., grey hair.
căpax, -ācis, ample, large.
căpella, -ae, f., she-goat.
căpillus, -i, m., hair.
căpĭo, -ĕre, cēpi, captum, take, catch, seize.
capto, -are, -āvi, -ātum, grasp at; strike up.
căput, ĭtis, n., head.
căreo, -ēre, -ui, -ĭtum, lack (+ abl.).
cărīna, -ae, f., keel; ship, vessel.

carpo, -ĕre, -psi, -ptum, pluck, pull off; consume, destroy (especially of emotion).
cārus, -a, -um, dear.
Castălĭus, -a, -um, Castalian.
cătēna, -ae, f., chain, fetter.
cauda, -ae, f., tail.
causa, -ae, f., cause, case, reason.
cēdo, -ĕre, cessi, cessum, yield, retreat.
cĕlĕber, -bris, -bre, famous.
cĕler, -ĕris, -ĕre, swift.
cēlo, -are, -āvi, -ātum, hide (trans.).
celsus, -a, -um, high.
census, -ūs, m., census, wealth, possessions.
centĭmănus, -a, -um, hundred-handed.
cēra, -ae, f., wax, wax figure.
Cĕrēs, -ĕris, f., (goddess of) corn, food.
cerno, -ĕre, crēvi, crētum, see.
certātim, emulously, eagerly.
certē, at any rate.
certus, -a, -um, sure; resolved.
cervix, -īcis, f., neck.
cervus, -i, m., stag.
cētĕrus, -a, -um, the rest.
ceu, as, like.
Chĭus, -a, -um, of Chios.
chŏrus, -i, m., dance.
cingo, -ĕre, -nxi, -nctum, surround, wrap, encircle.
circā, around.
circumdo, -ăre, -dĕdi, -dătum, surround, wrap, encircle.
circumfĕro, -ferre, -tŭli, -lātum, carry, cast round.
circumflŭo, -ĕre, -fluxi, flow round.
circumfundo, -ĕre, -fūdi, -fūsum, pour round (trans.).
circumlĭno, -ĕre, -lĭtum, smear all over.
circumsto, -are, -stĕti, stand round, surround.
cĭtus, -a, -um, quick, swift.
cīvĭlis, -e, civil, between citizens.
clādes, -is, f., disaster, misfortune.
clāmo, -are, -āvi, -ātum, shout, cry out.
clāmor, -ōris, m., shout.
clārus, -a, -um, clear, loud.
claudo, -ĕre, -si, -sum, close, enclose.

clĭpĕo, -are, -ātum, arm with a shield.

Cnōsius, -a, -um, Cnossian; Cretan.

cŏĕo, -ire, -ii (-ivi), -ĭtum, come together, meet; couple.

coepi, -isse, -tum, begin.

coetus, -ūs, m., assembly, crowd.

cognosco, -ĕre, -ōvi, -ĭtum, know, ascertain.

cōgo, -ĕre, coēgi, coactum, drive together; compel.

collĭgo, -ĕre, -lēgi, -lectum, gather.

collum, -i, n., neck.

cŏlo, -ĕre, -ui, cultum, cultivate; cherish, worship.

cŏlor, -ōris, m., colour; brightness.

cŏma, -ae, f., hair.

cŏmĕs, -ĭtis, m. or f., companion.

cŏmĭto, -are, -āvi, -ātum, accompany.

commĭniscor, -i, -mentus, invent, feign.

commĭnŭs, in close contest, hand to hand.

compāges, -is, f., joint, structure.

compello, -are, -āvi, -ātum, accost, address.

compendium, -ii, n., short cut.

complector, -i, -plexus, embrace.

compleo, -ēre, -ēvi, -ētum, fill; complete.

complexus, -ūs, m., embrace.

cōnāmen, -ĭnis, n., effort.

concĭĕo, -ēre, -īvi, -ĭtum, stir, urge, rouse.

concĭpio, -ĕre, -cēpi, -ceptum, take, receive; conceive.

concors, -dis, united.

condo, -ĕre, -dĭdi, -dĭtum, found, build; conceal.

confĕro, -ferre, -tŭli, collatum, bring together, join (trans.).

confĭtĕor, -ēri, -fessus, confess, acknowledge.

conĭcio, -ĕre, -iēci, -iectum, throw.

coniunx, -ŭgis, m. or f., husband, wife.

conscendo, -ĕre, -di, -sum, climb.

conscius, -a, -um, privy to, as a witness.

consīdĕro, -are, -āvi, -ātum, examine.

consisto, -ĕre, -stĭti, -stĭtum, stand still, remain, settle.

consŭlo, -ĕre, -ui, -tum, consult.

consūmo, -ĕre, -sumpsi, -sumptum, devour; spend.

contemno, -ĕre, -mpsi, -mptum, despise.

contemptor, -ōris, despiser.

contentus, -a, -um, content.

contingo, -ĕre, -tĭgi, -tactum, touch, reach; befall (intrans.).

contrăho, -ere, -xi, -ctum, draw together; narrow, lessen; wrinkle.

contrārius, -a, -um, opposite.

cōnus, -i, m., apex (of a helmet).

cōpia, -ae, f., abundance; means, power, opportunity.

cŏr, cordis, n., heart.

cornū, -ūs, n., horn.

cŏrōna, -ae, f., garland.

corpus, -ōris, n., body.

corrĭpio, -ĕre, -rĭpui, -reptum, seize, catch, take up; fascinate.

cŏrymbus, -i, m., cluster (of berries).

crēdo, -ĕre, -dĭdi, -dĭtum believe (+ dat.).

crēdulus, -a, -um, credulous.

creo, -are, -āvi, -ātum, create, bring forth.

cresco, -ĕre, crēvi, crētum, grow, increase.

crīmen, -ĭnis, n., charge; fault.

crīnis, -is, m., hair.

crista, -ae, f., crest.

crŏcĕus, -a, -um, rosy, yellow.

crūcio, -are, -āvi, -ātum, torture.

crūdēlis, -e, cruel.

cruento, -are, -āvi, -ātum, stain with blood.

cruentus, -a, -um, bloodstained.

crŭor, -ōris, m., blood, gore.

crūs, crūris, m., leg.

cultus, -ūs, appearance, dress.

culpo, -are, -āvi, -ātum, blame.

cum, when, since, though.

cūnae, -arum, f. pl., cradle.

cunctus, -a, -um, all.

cŭpīdo, -ĭnis, f., desire.

cŭpio, -ĕre, -ii (-ivi), -ītum, desire.

cŭpressus, -i or -ūs, f., cypress.

cūr, why?

cūra, -ae, f., care, concern; trouble, worry.

curro, -ĕre, cŭcurri, cursum, run, hurry.

cursus, -ūs, m., running; course.

curvāmen, -ĭnis, n., curve, bending.

curvo, -are, -āvi, -ātum, bend, curve (trans.).

curvus, -a, -um, bent, rounded; winding.

cuspis, -ĭdis, f., spear-tip, spear.

cŭtis, -is, f. skin.

Cyprius, -a, -um, of Cyprus.

D

damno, -are, -āvi, -ātum, condemn.

dea, -ae, f., goddess.

dēbeo, -ēre, -ui, -ĭtum, owe; ought.

dĕceo, -ēre, -ui, befit, suit.

decĭpio, -ĕre, -cēpi, -ceptum, deceive, snare, catch.

decurro, -ĕre, -cŭcurri (or -curri), -cursum, run down, flow down.

dĕcus, -ŏris, n., beauty; glory, honour.

dēdūco, -ĕre, -duxi, -ductum, draw down; unfurl.

dēfendo, -ĕre, -di, -sum, defend.

dēfĕro, -ferre, -tŭli, -lātum, bear, bring down, transport.

deĭcio, -ĕre, -iēci, -iectum, hurl down.

deĭndĕ, then.

dēlābor, -i, -lapsus, glide down, fly down.

dēlŭdo, -ĕre, -si, -sum, mock, deceive.

dēmens, -tis, mad, foolish.

dēmitto, -ĕre, -mīsi, -missum, send down, lower.

dēmo, -ĕre, dempsi, demptum, take away or off.

dēnĭque, at length.

dens, -tis, m., tooth, fang.

densus, -a, -um, thick, crowded.

dēpōno, -ĕre, -pŏsui, -pŏsĭtum, lay down, put off.

dēprendo, -ĕre, -i, -sum, seize, overtake, catch.

dērĭpio, -ĕre, -rĭpui, -reptum, tear from, snatch away.

dēscendo, -ĕre, -i, -sum, descend.

dēsĕro, -ĕre, -ui, -tum, desert.

dēsertus, -a, -um, lonely, deserted.

dēsĭlio, -ire, -ui, leap down.

dēspĭcio, -ĕre, -spexi, -spectum, look down on; despise.

dēsum, -esse, -fui be wanting (+ dat.).

dĕus, -i, m., god.

dēvĭus, -a, -um, unfrequented.

dexter, -ĕra (-ra), -ĕrum (-rum), right, on the right.

dextra, -ae, f., right hand.

dīco, -ĕre, -xi, -ctum, say, speak; call.

Dictaeus, -a, -um, Dictaean; Cretan.

dictum, -i, n., word.

diēs, -ēi, m. or f., day.

differo, differre, distŭli, dīlātum, separate; postpone.

diffĭcĭlis, -e, difficult.

diffundo, -ĕre, -fūdi, -fūsum, pour out, scatter; gladden.

dĭgĭtus, -i, m., finger.

dignor, -ari, -atus, think worthy.

dignus, -a, -um, worthy.

dīlăcĕro, -are, -āvi, -ātum, tear to pieces.

dīlĭgo, -ĕre, -lexi, -lectum, love.

dīmĭdius, -a, -um, half.

dīmitto, -ĕre, -mīsi, -missum, send out, away.

dīrĭpio, -ere, -rĭpŭi, -reptum, tear apart.

dīruo, -ĕre, -ui, -ŭtum, tear apart, destroy.

dīrus, -a, -um, terrible, awesome.

discēdo, -ĕre, -cessi, -cessum, depart.

disco, -ĕre, dĭdĭci, learn.

distinguo, -ere, -nxi, -nctum, separate, distinguish; adorn.

dīsto, -are, be distant.

diū, for a long time.

dĭŭturnus, -a, -um, long-lasting.

dīversus, -a, -um, contrary.

dīvus, -i, m., god.

do, dăre, dĕdi, dătum, give; cause; grant.

dare vela or lintea, set sail.

dare saltus, leap.

doctus, -a, -um, learned, skilled, experienced.

dŏleo, -ēre, -ui, -ĭtum, grieve.

dŏlor, ōris, m., pain, grief.

dŏmĭnus, -i, m., master, owner.

dŏmus, -ūs, f., house, home.
dōnĕc, until.
dōnum, -i, n., gift.
Drȳăs, -ădis, f., tree *or* wood nymph,
  Dryad.
dŭbĭto, -are, -āvi, -ātum, doubt;
  hesitate.
dūco, -ĕre, -xi, -ctum, lead, take;
  assume; form.
dum, while, until.
dŭŏ, -ae, -ŏ, two.
dūrĭtia, -ae, f., hardness.
dūro, -are, -āvi, -ātum, harden.
dūrus, -a, -um, hard, stubborn.
dux, dŭcis, m. *or* f., leader, guide.

E

ĕburnĕus, -a, -um, of ivory.
eccĕ, look!; suddenly.
ecquĭs, -quid, (is there) anyone
  (who?).
ēdo, -ĕre, -dĭdi, -dĭtum, give out,
  utter.
ēdŭco, -are, -āvi, -ātum, bring up.
ēdūco, -ĕre, -xi, -ctum, draw out.
effĕro, -ferre, extŭli, ēlatum,
  bring, carry out; put out; raise.
effĭcio, -ĕre, -fēci, -fectum, make,
  form, render.
efflo, -are, -āvi, -ātum, blow out,
  breathe out (trans.).
efflŭo, -ĕre, -xi, flow out; slip
  from.
ēgrĕdior, -i, -gressus, step out of,
  leave.
ĕhēu, alas!
ēlĭgo, -ĕre, -lēgi, -lectum, choose.
ēlŏquor, -i, -lŏcutus, declare.
ēmergo, -ĕre, -si, -sum, come out,
  emerge.
ēmĭnus, at *or* from a distance.
ēmŏrior, -i, -mortuus, die.
ēn, behold!
ēnītor, -i, -nīsus (-nixus), struggle
  out; bear (a child).
ensis, -is, m., sword.
ĕo, ire, ii (īvi), ĭtum, go.
Ēpĭdaurius, -a, -um, from Epidaurus.
ĕquus, -i, m., horse.
ergō, therefore.
ērĭgo, -ĕre, -rexi, -rectum, raise.

ĕrīlis, -e, of a master.
ērĭpio, -ĕre, -ui, -reptum, snatch
  away, pull out.
erro, -are, -āvi, -ātum, wander.
error, -ōris, m., wandering; mistake.
etsi, although.
ēvādo, -ĕre, -si, -sum, come out,
  through *or* past; escape.
ēvĕnio, -ire, -vēni, -ventum, come
  true.
excĭpio, -ĕre, -cēpi, -ceptum, take,
  receive, catch.
exclāmo, -are, -āvi, -ātum, cry out.
excŭtio, -ĕre, -cussi, -cussum, shake
  off.
exemplum, -i, n., example; manner.
exĕo, -ire, -ii (-ivi), -ĭtum, leave;
  rush out, escape.
exĭguus, -a, -um, small, narrow.
exĭlio, -ire, -ui, leap out.
exĭlium, -i, n., exile.
existo, -ĕre, -stĭti, -stĭtum, come
  forth; proceed.
exĭtus, -ūs, m., end.
expecto, -are, -āvi, -ātum, wait for.
expīro, -are, -āvi, -ātum, breathe
  out.
expleo, -ēre, -ēvi, -ētum, fill,
  complete; fulfil, discharge.
exprĭmo, -ĕre, -pressi, -pressum,
  push out.
exsurgo, -ĕre, -surrexi, rise.
extinguo, -ĕre, -nxi, -nctum, put
  out, destroy.
exto, -are, stand out *or* up.
extemplō, immediately.
extĕnŭo, -are, -āvi, -ātum, weaken.
extrĕmus, -a, -um, farthest.

F

făciēs, -ēi, f., form, face, beauty,
  appearance.
făcio, -ĕre, fēci, factum, do, make,
  perform, cause.
factum, -i, n., act, deed.
falcātus, -a, -um, sickle-shaped,
  curved.
fallax, -ācis, false, deceitful.
fallo, -ĕre, fĕfelli, falsum, deceive,
  cheat.
falsus, -a, -um, false.

fāma, -ae, f., fame, report.
fāmŭlus, -i, m., servant, attendant.
fātālis, -e, of fate, fated.
fāteor, -ēri, fassus, confess, acknowledge.
fātĭdĭcus, -a, -um, prophetic.
fātum, -i, n., fate.
fautrix, -īcis, f., guardian, patroness.
fāveo, -ēre, fāvi, fautum favour, delight in, comply (+ dat.).
fax, făcis, f., torch.
fēcundus, -a, -um, abounding in.
fēlix, -īcis, happy, fortunate.
fēmĭna, -ae, f., woman.
fēmĭnĕus, -a, -um, of women.
fĕmŭr, -ŏris, n., thigh.
fĕra, -ae, f., wild beast.
fĕrē, nearly, approximately.
fĕretrum, -i, n., bier.
fĕrio, -ire, strike.
fĕrĭtas, -ātis, f., fierceness.
fĕro, ferre, tŭli, lātum, bear, bring, offer; say.
fĕrox, -ōcis, brave, fierce.
ferrum, -i, n., iron; sword, blade, spear-tip.
fĕrus, -a, -um, savage, fierce.
ferveo, -ēre, ferbui, boil (intrans).
fessus, -a, -um, weary.
festus, -a, -um, merry, festive.
fīdes, -ĕi, f., faith, pledge.
fīdūcia, -ae, f., confidence.
fīdus, -a, -um, loyal, faithful.
fīgo, -ēre, fixi, fixum, fix, impress.
fīgūra, -ae, f., shape, figure.
findo, -ēre, fīdi, fissum, split, divide.
fīnio, -ire, -ii (-ivi), -ītum, end, limit.
fīnis, -is, m. or f., end.
fīo, fĭĕri, factus, become, be made.
fīrmo, -are, -āvi, -ātum, strengthen, confirm.
flăgello, -are, -āvi, -ātum, lash, beat.
flamma, -ae, f., flame.
flāvus, -a, -um, yellow, blonde.
flecto, -ēre, -xi, -xum, bend, turn (trans.).
fleo, -ēre, -ēvi, -ētum, weep.
flōs, -ōris, m., flower.

flūmĕn, -ĭnis, n., stream, river.
flŭo, -ēre, -xi, -xum, flow.
foedo, -are, -āvi, -ātum, stain, befoul.
foedus, -ēris, n., compact, union.
fŏlium, -i, n., leaf, petal.
fons, -tis, m., spring.
fŏris, -is, f., door.
forma, -ae, f., shape, beauty.
formo, -are, -āvi, -ātum, fashion, shape; influence.
formōsus, -a, -um, beautiful, shapely.
fortĕ, by chance, as it happens.
fortis, -e, strong, brave.
fortūna, -ae, fortune, luck; fate.
frāter, -tris, m., brother.
frāternus, -a, -um, of a brother, brotherly.
fraus, fraudis, f., deceit, trick; spell.
frĕmo, -ēre, -ui, -ītum, resound; roar, neigh.
frĕquento, -are, -āvi, -ātum, frequent; celebrate.
frīgus, -ŏris, n., cold.
frons, -dis, f., leaf.
frons, -tis, f., brow, forehead.
frustrā, in vain.
fŭga, -ae, f., flight.
fŭgax, -ācis, fleeting.
fŭgio, -ēre, fŭgi, flee, escape.
fulgor, -ōris, n., flash of lightning.
fulmĕn, -ĭnis, n., thunderbolt.
fulvus, -a, -um, yellow, golden.
fundo, -ēre, fūdi, fūsum, pour, spread out.
fūnestus, -a, -um, deadly.
fūnis, -is, m., rope.
fūnus, -ĕris, n., funeral rites.
fŭro, -ēre, rage, be furious.
fŭror, -ōris, m., madness.
furtim, by stealth.
furtum, -i, n., theft; a stolen thing; love affair.

G

gălĕa, -ae, f., helmet.
garrŭlus, -a, -um, talkative.
gaudeo, -ēre, gāvīsus, be glad.
gĕlĭdus, -a, -um, cold.
gĕmĭnus, -a, -um, twofold, twin.

gemmans, -ntis, sparkling with jewels.

gĕmo, -ĕre, -ui, -ĭtum, groan; bewail.

gĕna, -ae, f., cheek.

gĕnĕtīvus, -a, -um, original, given at birth.

gĕnĕtrix, -īcis, f., mother.

gens, -tis, f., nation, race.

gĕnū, -ūs, n., knee.

gĕnus, -ĕris, n., race, kind; descendants.

gĕro, -ĕre, gessi, gestum, bear; perform.

gigno, -ĕre, gĕnui, gĕnĭtum, bring forth, bear.

glaeba, -ae, f., clod of earth.

glōria, -ae, f., glory.

grădus, -ūs, m., step, stride, gait.

grāmen, -ĭnis, n., grass.

grāmĭneus, -a, -um, grassy.

grātēs, f. pl., thanks.

grăvĭdus, -a, -um, heavy; pregnant.

grăvis, -e, heavy.

gressus, -ūs, m., step.

grex, grĕgis, m., flock; crowd.

guttŭr, -ŭris, n., throat.

H

hăbeo, -ēre, -ui, -ĭtum, have, hold.

hăbĭto, -are, -āvi, -ātum, inhabit.

haereo, -ēre, haesi, haesum, cling, stick (intrans.).

hālĭtus, -ūs, m., breath.

hāmus, -i, m., hook.

hărēna, -ae, f., sand.

hasta, -ae, f., } spear.
hastīle, -is, n.,

haurio, -ire, hausi, haustum, draw off; snatch up.

hĕdĕra, -ae, f., ivy.

herba, -ae, f., grass.

hērēs, -ēdis, m. or f., heir.

hērōs, -ōis, m., hero.

hĭātus, -ūs, m., opening; basin (of spring).

hirsūtus, -a, -um, shaggy.

hŏmo, -ĭnis, m., man, human being.

hŏnor, -ōris , m., honour.

horrendus, -a, -um, dreadful, terrible.

hortātor, -ōris, m., encourager.

hortātus, -ūs, m., encouragement.

hospĕs, -ĭtis, m. or f., guest, stranger.

hospĭta, -ae, f. (as adj.), hospitable, friendly.

hostis, -is, m. or f., enemy.

hŭmĭlis, -e, low; poor.

hŭmus, -i, f., ground.

Hÿantius, -a, -um, Boeotian.

I

iăceo, -ēre, -ui, -ĭtum, lie.

iăcio, -ĕre, iēci, iactum, throw.

iacto, -are, -āvi, ātum, toss, fling; show off.

iăcŭlum, -i, n., javelin.

iamdūdum, for a long time past.

(īcio, -ĕre), īci, ictum, strike.

ictus, -ūs, m., stroke, blow; ray.

īdem, ĕădem, īdem, the same.

ignārus, -a, -um, ignorant.

ignis, -is, m., fire.

ignōtus, -a, -um, unknown, strange.

īlia, -ium, n. pl., belly, guts.

illĭmis, -e, without mud, clear.

illūdo, -ĕre, -si, -sum, play at or with; jeer, mock.

īmāgo, -ĭnis, f., image, semblance, appearance; echo.

imbĕr, -bris, m., rain, shower.

immensus, -a, -um, huge, measureless.

immisceo, -ēre, -ui, -mixtum, mix, intermingle (trans.).

immitto, -ĕre, -mīsi, -missum, send, let, cast into.

immōtus, -a, -um, motionless.

immūnis, -e, free from.

immurmŭro, -are, murmur at.

impĕdio, -ire, -ii (-ivi), -ĭtum, prevent, hinder.

impello, -ĕre, -pŭli, -pulsum, strike, push, drive.

imperfectus, -a, -um, incomplete, immature.

impĕro, -are, -āvi, -ātum command (+ dat.).

impĕtus, -ūs, m., attack, rush; force.

impius, -a, -um, wicked, godless.

impleo, -ēre, -plēvi, -ētum, fill.

implĭco, -are, -āvi or -ŭi, -ātum or

ĭtum, enfold.
impōno, -ĕre, -pŏsui, -pŏsĭtum, put on.
imprūdens, -ntis, unknowing.
impūbis, -is, beardless, smooth.
impulsus, -ūs, m., shock, pressure, force.
īmus, -a, -um, lowest, bottom.
ĭnānis, -e, empty; vain, unreal.
incălesco, -ĕre, -călui, grow hot; fall in love with.
incingo, -ĕre, -xi, -nctum, wrap, surround.
incĭpio, -ĕre, -cēpi, -ceptum, begin.
incĭto, -are, -āvi, -ātum, rouse, spur on.
incrēmentum, -i, n., growth; progeny, seed.
incrĕpo, -are, -ui, -ĭtum, blame, reproach.
incūnābŭla, -orum, n. pl., swaddling clothes, cradle.
incursus, -ūs, m., charge, attack.
incustōdītus, -a, -um, unguarded.
indĕ, thence; then.
indōlesco, -ĕre, -dōlui, grieve.
ĭnĕo, -ire, -ĭi, -ĭtum, enter, penetrate.
ĭnermis, -e, unarmed.
ĭnēvītābilis, -e, inescapable.
ĭnexplētus, -a, -um, unfilled, unsatisfied.
infans, -ntis, m. or f., baby, child.
infaustus, -a, -um, unfortunate, unlucky.
infēlix, -īcis, unhappy, unfortunate.
infĕro, -ferre, -tŭli, illātum, bring in.
infernus, -a, -um, of the underworld.
inficio, -ĕre, -fēci, -fectum, stain, pollute.
ingĕmino, -are, -āvi, -ātum, repeat, redouble.
ingĕmo, -ĕre, -gĕmui, groan.
ingĕnium, -i, n., nature, character; skill, genius.
ingens, -tis, huge, vast.
inhĭbeo, -ēre, -ui, -ĭtum, restrain, check.
ĭnĭcio, -ĕre, -iēci, -iectum, throw over, on.
iniūria, -ae, f., injury, wrong.

ĭnops, -ŏpis, destitute, poor.
Īnōus, -a, -um, of Ino.
inquam, -is, -it, say.
insānia, -ae, f., madness.
insānus, -a, -um, mad, crazed.
insĕro, -ĕre, -sĕrui, -sertum, put, bring, introduce into.
insignĕ, -is, n., badge, mark of rank.
instīgo, -are, -āvi, -ātum, urge, incite.
insto, -are, -stĭti, -stātum, stand on; press forward.
instrūmentum, -i, n., tool, instrument.
insŭo, -ĕre, -ŭi, -ūtum, sew up in.
intābesco, -ĕre, -bui, melt away.
interdum, sometimes.
intĕrĕo, -ire, -ii (-ivi), -ĭtum, perish.
intermitto, -ĕre, -mīsi, -missum, interrupt.
intexo, -ĕre, -ui, -xtum, weave into.
intorqueo, -ēre, -torsi, -tortum, twist, plait.
intro, -are, -āvi, -ātum, enter.
invĕho, -ĕre, -vexi, -vectum, carry in, transport.
invĕnio, -ire, -vēni, -ventum, find.
iŏcōsus, -a, -um, joking, playful.
iŏcus, -i, m. (also n. pl. ioca), joke.
īra, -ae, f., anger.
īrascor, -i, irātus, grow, be angry.
irrĕprēhensus, -a, -um, blameless.
irrīto, -are, -āvi, -ātum, excite, stimulate, inflame.
irrĭtus, -a, -um, of no effect, vain.
ĭtĕro, -are, -āvi, -ātum, repeat.
ĭtĕrum, again.
iŭbeo, -ēre, iussi, iussum, order.
iūdex, -ĭcis, m. or f., judge.
iŭgālis, -e, of marriage.
iŭgum, -i, n., yoke; ridge.
iŭrgium, -i, n., reproach.
iūro, -are, -āvi, -ātum, swear.
iūs, iūris, n., right, power.
iussum, -i, n., command.
iustum, -i, n., that which is right or just.
iustus, -a, -um, just, righteous.
iŭvĕnālis, -e, youthful.
iŭvenca, -ae, f., heifer.
iŭvencus, -i, m., bullock, steer.

126

iŭvĕnis, -is, m., youth, man, warrior.
iŭventūs, -ūtis, f., youth; young
men.
iŭvo, -are, iūvi, iūtum, help, assist;
delight.

L

lăbĕfăcio, -ĕre, -fēci, -factum,
make totter, shake.
lābor, -i, lapsus, slip, fall, glide.
lābor, -ōris, m., work.
lăbōro, -are, -āvi, -ātum, work,
strive; form, prepare.
lac, lactis, n., milk.
lăcer, -ĕra, -ĕrum, in pieces.
lăcĕro, -are, -āvi, -ātum, tear off
or in pieces.
lăcertus, -i, m., arm.
Lăcōnis, -ĭdis, f., Laconian, Spartan.
lăcrĭma, -ae, f., tear.
lăcrĭmo, -are, -āvi, -ātum, weep.
lăcus, -ūs, m., lake, pool.
laedo, -ĕre, -si, -sum, injure, wound.
laetus, -a, -um, joyful.
laevus, -a, -um, left.
lambo, -ĕre, -i, -ĭtum, lick.
lancea, -ae, f., spear, lance.
lānĭger, -ĕra, -ĕrum, fleecy.
lăpis, -ĭdis, m., stone.
lascīvus, -a, -um, playful, wanton.
lassus, -a, -um, weary.
lătĕbra, -ae, f., hiding-place.
lăteo, -ĕre, -ui, lie hid.
lătex, -ĭcis, m., liquid; water.
latrātus, -ūs, m., barking.
lătus, -ĕris, n., side, flank.
lātus, -a, -um, broad.
laudo, -are, -āvi, -ātum, praise.
lĕgo, -ĕre, lēgi, lectum, pick out,
choose; keep to.
lēnis, -e, smooth, gentle.
lentē, slowly.
lentus, -a, -um, slow; pliable.
lĕo, -ōnis, m., lion.
lēto, -are, -āvi, -ātum, slay.
lētum, -i, n., death.
lĕvis, -e, light, insubstantial,
small.
lĕvo, -are, -āvi, -ātum, lighten;
lift.
lex, lēgis, f., law.

lĭbenter, willingly, gladly.
lĭbet, -ēre, lĭbuit, lĭbĭtum (impers.
+ dat.), it is agreeable.
lībo, -are, -āvi, -ātum, pour out
(as an offering); draw from.
lĭcet, -ēre, lĭcuit or lĭcĭtum est
(impers. + dat.), it is allowed.
lĭgo, -are, -āvi, -ātum, bind, tie
together.
līmĕn, -ĭnis, n., threshold, door;
house.
lingua, -ae, f., tongue.
linteum, -i, n., linen; sail.
līnum, -i, n., thread, linen; net.
lĭquĕfacio, -ĕre, -fēci, -factum,
make clear, limpid.
lĭquĭdus, -a, -um, flowing, clear,
limpid.
līquor, -i, melt, dissolve (intrans.);
waste away.
līs, lītis, f., strife, dispute.
lītus, -ōris, n., shore.
lŏcus, -i, m., place (n. pl., lŏca).
longus, -a, -um, long.
lŏquor, -i, lŏcūtus, speak, say.
lōrīca, -ae, f., cuirass, corselet.
luctus, -ūs, m., grief.
lūcus, -i, m., sacred grove, wood.
lūdo, -ĕre, -si, -sum, play; make fun
of.
lūmen, -ĭnis, n., light; eye.
lūna, -ae, f., moon.
luo, -ĕre, lui, (1) wash; (2) atone
for, pay.
lŭpus, -i, m., wolf.
lustrum, -i, n., wilderness, wood.
lux, lūcis, f., light; day.
lympha, -ae, f., water.
lynx, -cis, m. or f., lynx.

M

măcies, -ēi, f., leanness.
măcŭlōsus, -a, -um, spotted, dappled.
mădeo, -ēre, -ŭi, be wet, drip.
mădĭdus, -a, -um, wet, dripping.
maestus, -a, -um, sad, mournful.
măgĭcus, -a, -um, magic.
magnus, -a, -um, great, big.
mălĕ, badly.
mălum, -i, n., evil, misfortune.

māneo, -ēre, -si, sum, remain, await.
mānifestus, -a, -um, clear, plain.
māno, -are, -āvi, -ātum, flow, trickle, drip.
mănus, -ūs, f., hand; band of men.
mărě, -is, n., sea.
margo, -ĭnis, m., edge, border.
marmor, -ŏris, n., marble.
marmŏreus, -a, -um, of, like marble.
Mars, -tis, m., (god of) war.
Martius, -a, -um, of Mars, sacred to Mars.
mās, māris, m. (adj. and subst.), male.
māter, ris, f., mother, matron.
mātĕria, -ae, f., subject, matter.
māternus, -a, -um, of a mother.
mātertĕra, -ae, f., mother's sister, aunt.
mātūrus, -a, -um, ripe.
mātūtĭnus, -a, -um, of the morning, early.
Māvortius, -a, -um, of Mars.
mĕdius, -a, -um, middle, midst of; medium, -i, n., middle.
membrum, -i, n., limb.
mĕmĭni, -isse, remember, recall.
mĕmor, -ŏris, mindful.
mĕmŏro, -are, -āvi, -ātum, tell, say.
mendax, -ācis, false, deceptive.
mens, -tis, f., mind, senses.
mĕreo, -ēre, -ui, -ĭtum, deserve.
mergo, -ēre, -si, -sum, plunge, sink.
mĕrum, -i, n., strong wine.
mēta, -ae, f., turning-point, goal; limit, end.
mĕtŭo, -ēre, -ŭi, -ūtum, fear.
mĕtus, -ūs, m., fear, dread.
mĭco, -are, -ui, flash, quiver.
millĕ (indecl.), thousand.
mĭna, -ae, f., threat.
mĭnister, -tri, m., servant, attendant.
mĭnistĕrium, -i, n., office, job, work.
mĭnor, -ari, -atus, threaten.
mĭnus, less.
mīrābĭlis, -e, wonderful, marvellous.
mīrācŭlum, -i, n., wonder, marvel.
mīror, -ari, -atus, wonder (at), admire.
misceo, -ēre, -ui, mixtum, mix.

mĭser, -ĕra, -ĕrum, } unhappy, wretched.
mĭsĕrābĭlis, -e,
mitto, -ēre, mīsi, missum, send, hurl; give out; cease.
mŏdĕrāmen, -ĭnis, n., restraint; steering.
mŏdĕro, -are, -āvi, -atum, regulate, control.
mŏdĭcus, -a, -um, moderate; little.
mŏdŏ, only; just, lately.
mŏdus, -i, m., manner; measure, beat.
moenia, -ium, n. pl., walls.
mōlāris, -is, m., large stone.
mollis, -e, soft, gentle, weak.
mŏneo, -ēre, -ui, -ĭtum, warn, advise.
mŏnĭtus, -ūs, m., warning, advice.
mons, -tis, m., mountain.
monstro, -are, -āvi, -ātum, show, point out.
mŏra, -ae, f., delay, long time.
mordeo, -ēre, mŏmordi, morsum, bite.
mŏrior, -i, mortuus, die.
mors, -tis, f., death.
morsus, -ūs, m., bite.
mortālis, -e, mortal, human.
mōs, mōris, m., custom, usage, fashion.
mōtus, -ūs, m., movement, motion.
mŏveo, -ēre, mōvi, mōtum, move, stir, rouse; touch.
mox, soon, afterwards, then.
mūgĭtus, -ūs, m., lowing.
multus, -a, -um, much, many.
mūnus, -ēris, gift.
murra, -ae, f., myrrh.
mūto, -are, -āvi, -ātum, change, exchange.
mūtuus, -a, -um, in exchange ; on or from each other.

N

Nāĭās, -ădis, f., } Naiad, water-nymph.
Nāĭs, -ĭdis, f.,
nanciscor, -i, nactus (nanctus), come upon, find.
nāris, -is, f., nostril, nose.
narro, -are, -āvi, -ātum, tell.
nascor, -i, nātus, be born;
nātus, -a, -um, child of;
natus, son;
nata, daughter.
nātīvus, -a, -um, natural.

nātūra, -ae, f., nature.
nauta, -ae, m., sailor.
nāvāle, -is, n., dockyard.
nē, lest, not (in prohibitions).
nĕco, -are, -āvi, -ātum, kill.
nectar, -ăris, n., nectar.
nĕfandus, -a, -um, unspeakable,
   abominable.
nĕgo, -are, -āvi, -ātum, deny.
nēmo, no one.
nĕmŏrālis, -e, wooded.
nĕmus, -ŏris, n., wood, grove.
nĕpos, -ōtis, m., grandson.
nescio, -ire, -ii (-ivi), -ītum, not
   to know.
nex, nĕcis, f., violent death.
nexus, -ūs, m., coil, fold, entwining.
nĭger, -ra, -rum, black.
nĭgresco, -ĕre, -grui, grow black.
nĭhil or nil, nothing.
nimbus, -i, m., thunder-cloud.
nĭmium, too much.
nĭsĭ, unless, if not.
nĭtĭdus, -a, -um, sparkling.
nĭtor, -i, nixus (nīsus), lean;
   strive.
nĭveus, -a, -um, snow-white.
nŏceo, -ēre, -ui, -ītum, do harm,
   injure (+ dat.),
nōdōsus, -a, -um, knotted.
nōdus, -i, m., knot.
nōmen, -ĭnis, n., name.
nondum, not yet.
nosco, -ĕre, nōvi, nōtum, know, re-
   cognize;
   nōtus, -a, -um, well-known.
nŏto, -are, -āvi, -ātum, mark, ob-
   serve.
nŏvĭtas, -ātis, f., novelty.
nŏvus, -a, -um, new; strange.
nox, noctis, f., night.
nūbēs, -is, f., cloud.
nūbĭla, -ōrum, n. pl., clouds.
nŭdus, -a, -um, naked.
nullus, -a, -um, none, no.
nūmen, -ĭnis, n., deity, divine power.
nŭmĕrus, -i, m., number.
numquam, never.
nūper, lately.
nŭrus, -ūs, f., daughter-in-law.
nusquam, nowhere.
nūto, -are, -āvi, -ātum, nod.

nutrix, -īcis, f., nurse.
nūtus, -ūs, m., nod.
nympha, -ae (or nymphē, -ēs), f.,
   nymph.
Nȳsēis, -ĭdis, f., of Mt. Nysa.

O

ōbex, ōbicis, m. or f., bar, obstruc-
   tion.
ōbĭcio, -ere, -iēci, -iectum, throw
   to; taunt, reproach with.
ōbĭtus, -ūs, m., death.
oblīquus, -a, -um, sideways, slanting.
obscēnus, -a, -um, ill-omened, hate-
   ful; impure.
obscūrus, -a, -um, dark, blurred.
obsĕquium, -i, n., obedience, com-
   pliance.
obsisto, -ĕre, -stĭti, -stĭtum, set
   one's self before, oppose.
obsto, -āre, -stĭti, -stātum, hinder,
   resist (+ dat.).
obstrŭo, -ĕre, -struxi, -structum,
   put in the way.
obstŭpesco, -ĕre, -pui, be astounded.
obverto, -ĕre, -ti, -sum, turn towards,
   up; ship (oars).
occŭlo, -ĕre, -cŭlui, -cultum, cover,
   hide.
occŭpo, -are, -āvi, -ātum, seize; be
   the first to.
occurro, -ĕre, curri, cursum, meet
   (+ dat.).
ócĭor, ōcius, swifter.
octāvus, -a, -um, eighth.
ŏcŭlus, -i, m., eye.
ŏdĭum, -i, n., hate.
offĕro, -ferre, obtŭli, oblātum, bring
   before, offer.
Ōlĕnius, -a, -um, belonging to Olenos;
   hence Achaean, Aetolian.
omnĭpŏtens, -ntis, almighty.
omnis, -e, all, every.
ŏnĕro, -are, -āvi, -ātum, burden,
   load.
ŏpācus, -a, -um, shady, dark; thick.
opportūnus, -a, -um, fit, opportune.
opprĭmo, -ĕre, -pressi, -pressum,
   close, stop up.
(ops), ŏpis, f., help; (pl.) wealth.

opto, -are, -āvi, -ātum, pray, wish (for).
ŏpus, -ĕris, n., work, task.
ōra, -ae, f., edge, border, shore.
ōrācŭlum, -i, n., oracle.
orbis, -is, m., circle, orb; world, region.
orbus, -a, -um, bereft of.
ordo, -ĭnis, m., row, order.
ŏrior, -īri, ortus, rise, spring from.
ōro, -are, -āvi, -ātum, pray, entreat.
ōs, ōris, n., face, mouth, lips.
ŏs, ossis, n., bone.
oscŭlum, -i, n., mouth, kiss.
ostendo, -ĕre, -di, -sum (-tum), show.

P

paelex, -ĭcis, f., concubine, mistress.
pălātum, -i, n., palate.
palla, -ae, f., cloak.
palma, -ae, f., palm, hand.
pampĭnĕus, -a, -um, full of (vine) tendrils.
pandus, -a, -um, curved, bent.
panthēra, -ae, f., panther.
păr, păris, equal, like.
părens, -entis, m. or f., parent.
păreo, -ēre, -ui, obey (+ dat.).
părĭter, equally; at the same time.
Părĭus, -a, -um, of Paros.
păro, -are, -āvi, -ātum, prepare (trans.).
pars, -tis, f., part, side, direction; some.
partĭceps, -ĭpis, sharing in.
parvus, -a, -um, little, small.
pascor, -i, pastus, graze.
passus, -ūs, m., step.
pastor, -ōris, m., shepherd.
pătĕfăcio, -ĕre, -fēci, -factus, open, reveal.
păteo, -ēre, -ui, lie open, be revealed.
păter, -tris, m., father.
păternus, -a, -um, of a father.
pătior, -i, passus, bear, suffer; allow.
pătria, -ae, f., native land, country.

pătrius, -a, -um, of a father.
pătŭlus, -a, -um, broad, spreading.
paulātim, gradually, little by little.
paulum, a little.
pauper, -ĕris, poor.
păvĭdus, -a, -um, trembling, terrified.
păvor, -ōris, m., trembling, fear.
pax, pācis, f., peace.
pecco, -are, -āvi, -ātum, err, do wrong.
pectus, -ōris, n., breast.
pĕcus, -ŭdis, f., beast, animal.
pĕcus, -ŏris, n., cattle, herd, flock.
pellis, -is, f., skin, hide.
pello, -ĕre, pĕpŭli, pulsum, drive back, rout.
pĕnātes, -ium, m. pl., household gods.
pĕnētro, -are, -āvi, -ātum, reach.
percŭtio, -ĕre, -cussi, -cussum, strike, beat, gone.
perdo, -ĕre, -dĭdi, -dĭtum, lose; destroy.
pĕrēgrīnus, -a, -um, foreign.
pĕreo, -ire, -ii (-ivi), -ĭtum, perish.
pĕrerro, -are, -āvi, -ātum, wander through or over.
perfundo, -ĕre, -fūdi, -fūsum, pour over, bathe.
pĕrimo, -ĕre, -ēmi, -emptum, destroy, kill.
perlūcĭdus, -a, -um, transparent.
perlŭo, -ĕre, -lui, -lūtum, wash, bathe.
perpĕtior, -i, -pessus, suffer; allow.
perquīro, -ĕre, -sīvi, -sītum, search for.
persto, -are, -stĭti, -stātum, persist.
pervĕnio, -ire, vēni, -ventum, come to, reach.
pēs, pĕdis, m., foot.
pestĭfer, -ĕra, -ĕrum, deadly, baleful.
pĕto, -ĕre, -ivi (-ii), -ītum, seek, ask; aim at.
phăretra, -ae, f., quiver.
phăretrātus, -a, -um, quiver-bearing.
Phoebēus, -a, -um, of Apollo.
pĭcĕa, -ae, f., pine.
pignus, -ōris, f., pledge.
pingo, -ĕre, -nxi, pictum, paint; embroider.
pinna, -ae, f., fin.

pīnus, -ūs (-i), f., pine; ship.

piscis, -is, m., fish.

pius, -a, -um, pious, dutiful; loyal; loving (towards gods, family or country).

plăceo, -ēre, -ui, -ĭtum, please, seem good (+ dat.).

plăcĭdus, -a, -um, calm, even, steady.

plāga, -ae, f., blow.

plango, -ēre, -nxi, -nctum, strike; beat the head, breast in grief, mourn.

plangor, -ōris, m., beating; mourning (cf. plango).

plēbs, -is, f., common people.

plēnus, -a, -um, full.

plūs, more.

plŭvĭālis, -e, rainy.

poena, -ae, f., punishment, penalty.

pōmum, -i, n., fruit, apple.

pondus, -ĕris, n., weight.

pōno, -ĕre, pŏsui, pŏsĭtum, place, put; lay aside.

pontus, -i, m., sea.

pŏpŭlus, -i, m., people, nation.

porrĭgo, -ĕre, -rexi, -rectum, stretch, hold out.

porta, -ae, f., gate.

portus, -ūs, m., harbour.

possum, posse, potui, can, be able.

post, after, behind.

postquam, after, when.

pŏtens, -ntis, powerful, influential.

pŏtentia, -ae, f., power.

pŏtestās, -ātis, f., power; use.

pŏtior, -iri, -ītus, gain possession of (+ abl.).

praebeo, -ēre, -ui, -ĭtum, offer, furnish, give.

praeceps, -ĭpĭtis, headlong.

praecĭpĭto, -are, -āvi, -ātum, throw down, rush down; hasten.

praeda, -ae, f., booty, spoils.

praenuntius, -a, -um, foretelling.

praesāgus, -a, -um, prophetic.

praesens, -tis, present; powerful, auspicious.

praesignis, -e, remarkable, distinguished.

praestans, -tis, distinguished, excellent.

praetendo, -ēre, -di, -tum, stretch forward, hold in front.

praeter (+ acc.), except, besides.

praevălĭdus, -a, -um, very strong.

prĕcor, -ari, -atus, pray.

prĕhendo, -ēre, -di, -sum, seize, grasp.

prĕmo, -ēre, pressi, pressum, press; form; contract.

(prex), prĕcis, f., prayer, entreaty.

prīmus, -a, -um, first; earliest.

prior, -ōris, former.

pristĭnus, -a, -um, former, early.

pro (+ abl.), for, on behalf of; in proportion to; instead of.

prŏbo, -are, -āvi, -ātum, prove, approve.

prŏcer, -ĕris, m., chief.

procumbo, -ĕre, -cŭbŭi, -ĭtum, sink down.

prŏcul, at a distance, far.

prŏfānus, -a, -um, unholy, uninitiated.

prŏfecto, certainly.

proficio, -ĕre, -fēci, -fectum, achieve, gain.

prŏfĭciscor, -i, prŏfectus, set out, depart; spring from.

prŏfŭgus, -a, -um, exiled.

prŏhibeo, -ēre, -ui, -ĭtum, forbid, prevent, keep apart.

prōles, -is, f., offspring.

prōmitto, -ere, -mīsi, -missum, promise.

promptus, -a, -um, ready, at hand; easy.

prōnus, -a, -um, bent forward.

prŏpĕro, -are, -āvi, -ātum, hasten.

prŏpior, -us, nearer.

prŏpōno, -ĕre, -pŏsŭi, -pŏsĭtum, intend.

prōra, -ae, f., prow.

prospecto, -are, -āvi, -ātum, look out on, behold.

prospĭcio, -ĕre, -spexi, -spectum, look out.

protĕgo, -ĕre, -xi, -ctum, protect, hide.

prōtĭnŭs, immediately.

prōturbo, -are, -āvi, -ātum, push away or through.

proximus, -a, -um, nearest, next (to).

prūdens, -ntis, knowing.

prŭīna, -ae, f., hoar-frost.
pŭdĭbundus, -a, -um, bashful, modest.
pŭdīcus, -a, -um, chaste.
pŭdor, -ōris, m., shame.
puella, -ae, f., girl.
puer, -i, m., boy.
pugna, -ae, f., battle.
pugnus, -i, m., fist.
pulcher, -chra, -chrum, beautiful.
pūmex, -ĭcis, m., pumice stone.
puppis, -is, f., stern; ship.
purpŭra, -ae, f., purple (cloth).
purpŭreus, -a, -um, purple.
pūrus, -a, -um, clean, pure; free from.
pŭto, -are, -āvi, -ātum, think, suppose.

Q

quā, where; quācumque, wherever.
quaero, -ĕre, -sīvi, -sītum, ask; seek.
quālis, -e, such as, as.
quamquam and quamvīs, although.
quantus, -a, -um, how great, as great as; quantum, as great as.
quătio, -ĕre, quassum, shake.
quercus, -ūs, f., oak.
quĕrēla, -ae, f., complaint.
quĕror, -i, questus, complain (of).
quia, because.
quĭdem, indeed.
quiēs, -ētis, f., rest, sleep.
quīni, -ae, -a, five each, five.
quisquam, quaequam, quicquam, any.
quisquis, quodquod (quicquid), whoever, whatever.
quo, whither.
quondam, once.
quŏt, indecl., how many, as many as.
quŏtiens, how often, as often as.

R

răbĭes, -ēi, f., madness, rage.
răcemĭfer, -ĕra, -ĕrum, cluster-bearing.
răcēmus, -i, m., cluster.
rādo, -ĕre, -si, -sum, scrape, rub, graze.

rāmus, -i, m., branch, bough.
răpĭdus, -a, -um, swift.
răpio, -ĕre, -ui, -ptum, seize, catch, carry off; hasten.
raptus, -ūs, m., carrying off; rending.
rătis, -is, f., boat.
rătus, -a, -um (from reor), established, valid, sure.
rĕcandesco, -ĕre, -dui, grow white; grow hot again.
rĕcens, -tis, new, fresh.
rĕcessus, -ūs, m., recess.
rĕcĭpio, -ĕre, -cēpi, -ceptum, receive; take back.
rĕconditus, -a, -um, hidden.
rectus, -a, -um, straight, upright.
rĕcurvus, -a, -um, bent back; winding.
reddo, -ĕre, -dĭdi, -dĭtum, give back; answer; make, render.
rĕdeo, -ire, -ii, -ĭtum, return (intrans.).
rĕdūco, -ĕre, -xi, -ctum, draw, bring back.
rĕfĕro, -ferre, rettŭli, relātum, bring back; relate, repeat; turn.
rĕfŭgio, -ĕre, -fūgi, flee, shrink back.
rēgālis, -e, royal.
rēgĭmen, -ĭnis, n., rudder.
rēgĭna, -ae, f., queen.
rĕlābor, -i, -lapsus, slide, slip back, down.
rĕlinquo, -ĕre, -līqui, -lictum, leave.
rĕmăneo, -ĕre, -nsi, remain.
rĕmitto, -ĕre, -mīsi, -missum, send back; rĕmissus, -a, -um, loose; happy, relaxed.
rĕmŏveo, -ĕre, -mōvi, -mōtum, remove, withdraw (trans.).
rēmus, -i, m., oar.
rĕpandus, -a, -um, bent back, crooked.
rĕpello, -ĕre, reppŭli, rĕpulsum, drive back, repulse; strike.
rĕpercŭtio, -ĕre, -cussi, -cussum, strike back, reflect.
rĕpĕto, -ĕre, -ii (-ivi), -ītum, seek again; renew.

repleo, -ēre, -ēvi, -ētum, fill.
rēporto, -are, -āvi, -ātum, bring
back, give back.
rēpugno, -are, -āvi, -ātum, oppose,
resist.
rēpulsa, -ae, f., rebuff.
rēquies, -ētis, f., rest.
rēquiesco, -ēre, -ēvi, -ētum, rest,
repose.
rēquiro, -ēre, -sīvi, -sītum, seek
for; seek to know, ask.
rēs, rēi, f., thing, affair.
res secundae, good fortune, prosperity.
rēsilio, -ire, -ui, leap back;
shrink, contract.
rēsōnābilis, -e, ⎫ resounding, re-
rēsōnus, -a, -um, ⎭ echoing.
rēsōno, -are, -āvi, resound.
respicio, -ēre, -spexi, -spectum,
look back (at), round.
rēspondeo, -ēre, -di, -sum, answer.
rēsponsum, -i. n., answer, reply.
resto, -are, -stīti, stand still,
remain.
rēsupīnus, -a, -um, turned upwards.
rētardo, -are, -āvi, -ātum, keep
back, hinder.
rētē, -is, n., net.
rētendo, -ēre, -di, -tum (-sum),
loosen, unbend.
rēticeo, -ēre, -ui, keep silence.
rētineo, -ēre, -ui, -tentum, hold,
keep back.
rētorqueo, -ēre, -si, -tum, bend,
twist back.
rētrāho, -ēre, -xi, -ctum, draw back.
retro, back.
rēvincio, -ire, -nxi, -nctum, bind
back, bind fast.
rīctus, -ūs, m., gaping jaws.
rīdeo, -ēre, rīsi, rīsum, laugh,
laugh at.
rīgeo, -ēre, -ui, be stiff, bristle.
rīgidus, -a, -um, stiff, hard.
rītē, duly, rightly.
rōbur, -ōris, n., oak; strength.
rōgo, -are, -āvi, -ātum, ask, entreat.
rōgus, -i, m., funeral pile.
rōro, -are, -āvi, -ātum, drop (trans.);
trickle, drip (intrans.).

rōs, rōris, m., dew; water.
rōsēus, -a, -um, rosy.
rostrum, -i, n., beak; muzzle, mouth.
rōta, -ae, f., wheel.
rūbeo, -ēre, be red.
rūbesco, -ēre, -bui, grow red.
rūbor, -ōris, m., redness, red.
rūdens, -tis, m., rope, sheet.
rūga, -ae, f., wrinkle.
rūmor, -ōris, m., report, rumour.
rumpo, -ēre, rūpi, ruptum, break,
crush.
ruo, -ēre, rui, rūtum, rush.
rūpēs, -is, f., rock, crag.
rursus, again.
rūs, rūris, n., country.

S

sācer, -ra, -rum, sacred, holy.
sacrum, -i, n., rite, sacrifice.
saecūlum, -i, n., age, generation.
saepe, often.
saevitia, -ae, f., ferocity, violence.
saevus, -a, -um, fierce, savage.
sāgax, -ācis, keen-scented.
sāgitta, -ae, f., arrow.
sālio, -ire, salui, leap.
saltus, -ūs, m., leap.
sālūs, -ūtis, f., safety.
sāluto, -are, -āvi, -ātum, greet.
sanctus, -a, -um, holy.
sanguinēus, -a, -um, blood-stained.
sanguis, -inis, m., blood.
sānus, -a, -um, of sound mind.
sātio, -are, -āvi, -ātum, satisfy,
glut.
sātis, enough.
saucius, -a, -um, wounded.
saxum, -i, n., rock, stone.
scēlērātus, -a, -um, wicked, guilty.
scēlus, -ēris, n., crime.
sceptrum, -i, n., sceptre.
scīlicet, of course, doubtless.
scio, -ire, -īvi, -ītum, know.
scōpūlus, -i, m., rock, cliff.
sēcēdo, -ēre, -cessi, -cessum, go
apart, withdraw.
sēco, -are, -ui, -ctum, cut.
sēcundus, -a, -um, second; favourable,
prosperous.
sēcūris, -is, f., axe.

sĕdeo, -ēre, sēdi, sessum, sit, settle in; penetrate.

sēdes, -is, f., seat; home.

sēdo, -are, -āvi, -ātum, soothe, slake.

sēdūco, -ēre, -xi, -ctum, draw aside, separate.

sĕgĕs, -ĕtis, f., crop.

segnis, -e, late, lingering; sluggish.

Sĕmēlēĭus, -a, -um, of Semele.

sēmen, -ĭnis, n., seed.

semper, always.

sĕnecta, -ae, f., old age.

sĕnex, sĕnis, m., old man.

sensus, -ūs, m., sense, feeling.

sententia, -ae, f., opinion, verdict.

sentio, -ire, sensi, sensum, feel, perceive.

sēpăro, -are, -āvi, -ātum, separate.

sēpōno, -ēre, -pŏsui, -pŏsitum, lay aside.

sēquor, -i, sĕcūtus, follow.

sermo, -ōnis, m., talk, conversation.

serpens, -tis, m. or f., snake, dragon.

serpo, -ēre, -psi, -ptum, creep; wind.

servĭtium, -i, n., slavery.

sĕvērus, -a, -um, stern, austere.

sībĭla, -ōrum, n. pl., hiss.

siccus, -a, -um, dry.

sīcŭt, just as.

Sĭcyōnius, -a, -um, of Sicyon.

Sĭdōnius, -a, -um, from Sidon; Phoenician.

sīdus, -ēris, n., star.

signĭfĭco, -are, -āvi, -ātum, make known, intimate.

signum, -i, n., mark; signal; image, picture, figure, statue.

silva, -ae, f., wood, forest.

sĭmĭlis, -e, like.

sĭmŭl, at the same time; (conj.) as soon as.

sĭmŭlacrum, -i, n., image, semblance.

sĭmŭlo, -are, -āvi, -ātum, feign, imitate.

sĭnĕ (+ abl.), without.

sĭno, -ēre, sīvi, sĭtum, allow.

sĭnuo, -are, -āvi, -ātum, wind, bend, curve.

sisto, -ēre, stĕti or stĭti, place; halt, cease.

sĭtis, -is, f., thirst.

sīve, whether, or.

sŏcer, -ĕri, m., father-in-law.

sŏcius, -i, m., comrade.

sōl, sōlis, m., sun.

sŏleo, -ēre, -ĭtus, be accustomed; sŏlĭtus, -a, -um, accustomed, habitual.

sŏlĭdus, -a, -um, solid, strong.

sŏlĭum, -i, n., throne.

sōlus, -a, -um, alone, lonely, deserted.

solvo, -ēre, -vi, sŏlūtum, loosen, set free.

somnus, -i, m., sleep.

sŏnĭtus, -ūs, m., sound.

sŏno, -are, -ui, -ĭtum, make a sound.

sŏnus, -i, m., sound.

sŏpor, -ōris, m., sleep, stupor.

sŏror, -ōris, f., sister.

sors, -tis, f., lot; condition, sex; oracle.

sortior, -iri, -ītus, draw, receive by lot.

spargo, -ēre, -rsi, -rsum, sprinkle, scatter.

Spartānus, -a, -um, of Sparta.

spătĭōsus, -a, -um, big, wide.

spătium, -i, n., space, extent; length.

spĕcĭes, -ēi, f., appearance, form.

spĕcĭōsus, -a, -um, handsome, brilliant.

spectābĭlis, -e, open to view.

spectāculum, -i, n., sight, show.

specto, -are, -āvi, -ātum, see, look at, watch.

spĕcus, -ūs, m., cave.

sperno, -ēre, sprēvi, sprētum, scorn.

spēro, -are, -āvi, -ātum, hope.

spēs, -ēi, f., hope.

spīna, -ae, f., thorn; backbone, back.

spīra, -ae, f., coil, fold, twist.

splendeo, -ēre, shine, glitter.

spŏlium, -i, n., spoil, plunder.

sponte, of one's own accord.

spūma, -ae, f., foam.

spūmeus, -a, -um, foaming.

squāma, -ae, f., scale.

squāmōsus, -a, -um, scaly.

stīpo, -are, -āvi, -ātum, surround, press round.

stirps, -pis, f., stock, race.

sto, stare, stĕti, stătum, stand, stand still.

strĕpĭtus, -ūs, m., noise.

stringo, -ĕre, -inxi, -ictum, draw (weapon).

stŭdium, -i, n., desire, eagerness; pursuit.

stŭpeo, -ēre, -ui, be amazed, aghast.

Stygĭus, -a, -um, of Styx.

sŭb (+ acc. or abl.), under, beneath.

sŭbeo, -ire, -ii (-īvi), -ĭtum, go under; approach, come up (to).

sŭbĭcio, -ĕre, -iēci, -iectum, put under.

sŭbĭto, suddenly.

sŭbĭtus, -a, -um, sudden; newly made.

subsĕquor, -i, subsĕcūtus, follow close after.

substrictus, -a, -um, contracted, narrow.

successor, -ōris, m., follower, successor.

succingo, -ĕre, -nxi, -nctum, hitch up.

sūcus, -i, m., moisture, sap; vigour.

sulco, -are, -āvi, -ātum, furrow.

sulcus, -i, m., furrow.

sulphur, -ŭris, n., sulphur, brimstone.

summitto, -ĕre, -mīsi, -mīssum, lower, let down.

summus, -a, -um, highest, top of.

sūmo, -ĕre, -mpsi, -mptum, take up, undertake; choose.

sŭperbia, -ae, f., haughtiness, pride.

sŭperēmĭneo, -ēre, overtop, rise above.

sŭpero, -are, -āvi, -ātum, remain.

sŭperstĕs, -ĭtis, surviving.

sŭpersum, -esse, -fui, be left over, remain.

sŭperus, -a, -um, upper, higher; sŭperi, -ōrum, m. pl., the gods.

supplex, -ĭcis, m., suppliant.

suppōno, -ĕre, -pŏsui, -pŏsitum, place, set under.

suprā, above, over, beyond.

suprēmus, -a, -um, highest, last.

surgo, -ĕre, surrexi, surrectum, rise.

suspĭcor, -ari, -atus, suspect.

suspiro, -are, -āvi, -ātum, sigh.

sustĭneo, -ēre, -ui, -tentum, hold up, check; sustain, maintain.

sŭsurro, -are, mutter, whisper.

T

tābēs, -is, f., wasting away, decay, corruption.

tābesco, -ĕre, -ui, waste away.

tăcĭturnus, -a, -um, silent.

tăcĭtus, -a, -um, silent.

taeda, -ae, f., torch.

tālis, -e, such.

tămĕn, yet, nevertheless.

tamquam, as if, just as.

tango, -ĕre, tĕtĭgi, tactum, touch; set foot on.

tantus, -a, -um, so great;

tantum, only.

tardus, -a, -um, slow.

taurus, -i, m., bull.

tectum, -i, n., roof, house, dwelling.

tegimen (tegmen), -ĭnis, covering.

tĕgo, -ĕre, texi, tectum, cover, hide.

tellūs, -ūris, f., earth, land.

tēlum, -i, n., weapon, spear.

templum, -i, n., temple.

tempŏra, -um, n. pl., temples, brows.

temptāmĕn, -ĭnis, n., test, trial.

tempto, -are, -āvi, -ātum, attempt, try.

tempus, -ōris, n., time.

tendo, -ĕre, tĕtendi, tentum, stretch.

tĕnĕbrae, -arum, f. pl., darkness; blindness.

tĕneo, -ēre, -ui, tentum, hold, maintain; steer for; occupy.

tĕner, -ĕra, -ĕrum, delicate, young.

tĕnor, -ōris, m., motion, course.

tĕnuis, -e, thin, slight; shallow.

tĕnuo, -are, -āvi, -ātum, make thin.

tĕnus (+ abl.), as far as, by.

tĕpeo, -ēre, be warm.

tĕpesco, -ĕre, -ui, grow warm.

tĕpĭdus, -a, -um, warm.

ter, three times.

tergum, -i, n., back.

terra, -ae, f., earth, land, country.

terreo, -ēre, -ui, -ĭtum, frighten, terrify.

terrĭgĕnus, -a, -um, born from the earth.

terror, -ōris, m., fright, terror.

thălămus, -i, m., bridal chamber; marriage.

thĕātrum, -i, n., theatre.

thyrsus, -i, m., Bacchic wand.

tībia, -ae, f., pipe.

tigris, -is (-ĭdis), m. or f., tiger.

tĭmeo, -ēre, -ui, fear, be afraid.

tĭmor, -ōris, m., fear.

tĭngo, -ēre, -nxi, -nctum, dye, wet.

tĭtŭbo, -are, -āvi, -ātum, totter, reel.

tōfus, -i, m., tufa (volcanic rock).

tollo, -ĕre, sustŭli, sublātum, raise, lift, take away.

tŏnĭtrus, -us, m., thunder.

tormentum, -i, n., engine of war; rack, torture.

torqueo, -ēre, -si, -tum, twist, roll; hurl.

torrens, -entis, m., torrent.

tŏt, so many;

tŏtidem, just as many;

tŏtiens, so often.

tōtus, -a, -um, whole.

trabs, trăbis, f., beam, plank; tree.

trādo, -ĕre, -dĭdi, -dĭtum, hand over, give.

trăho, -ĕre, -xi, -ctum, draw, bring; take on, assume.

transfero, -ferre, -tŭli, -lātum, transfer, shift.

trĕmo, -ĕre, -ui, tremble;

trĕmendus, -a, -um, fearful, terrible.

trĕmor, -ōris, m., trembling.

trĕpĭdus, -a, -um, frightened, startled.

trĭplex, -ĭcis, threefold, triple.

tristis, -e, sad, gloomy; grievous.

truncus, -a, -um, disfigured, limbless.

trux, trŭcis, fierce, savage.

tŭba, -ae, f., trumpet.

tŭbĭcen, -ĭnis, m., trumpeter.

tŭmeo, -ēre, -ui, swell.

tŭmultus, -ūs, m., uproar, storm.

tŭmŭlus, -i, m., mound.

turba, -ae, f., crowd, number.

turbo, -are, -āvi, -ātum, trouble, disturb.

turris, -is, f., tower.

tūs, tūris, n., incense.

Tuscus, -a, -um, Etruscan.

tūtēla, -ae, f., watching, protection; guardian, watcher.

tūtus, -a, -um, safe.

tympănum, -i, n., drum, tambourine.

Tўrius, -a, -um, of Tyre; Phoenician.

Tyrrhēnus, -a, -um, Etruscan; Lydian.

U

ūber, -ĕris, fruitful, plentiful.

ūdus, -a, -um, wet.

ullus, -a, -um, any.

ultĕrius, adv., further, longer.

ultĭmus, -a, -um, last, furthest, extreme.

ultor, -ōris, m., avenger.

ultrix, -īcis, f. adj., avenging.

ultro, of one's own accord; too, besides.

ŭlŭlātus, -ūs, m., wail, shriek, howl.

ūlŭlo, -are, -āvi, -ātum, shriek, howl.

umbra, -ae, f., shade; image, semblance.

ŭmĕrus, -i, m., shoulder.

ūmor, -ōris, m., moisture.

umquam, ever.

unda, -ae, f., wave; water.

undĕ, whence.

undĭquĕ, on or from all sides.

ūnĭcus, -a, -um, sole, single; unparalleled.

ūnus, -a, -um, one, alone.

urbs, -bis, f., city.

urna, -ae, f., jug.

ūro, -ĕre, ussi, ustum, burn, consume by fire.

usquĕ, all the way to, as far as; always.

ūsus, -ūs, m., use.

ŭt, conj. (1) final, in order that;
(2) consecutive, so that, namely that;
(3) temporal, when; (4) comparative,

as; (5) *concessive*, ut ... sic,
though ... *yet*.
ŭterque, utrăque, utrumque, each of
two, both.
ŭtĕrus, -i, *m.*, womb.
ūtĭlis, -e, useful.
ŭtĭnam, would that *(in wishes)*.
ūva, -ae, *f.*, grape.

V

văcuus, -a, -um, empty, devoid of;
at leisure.
vādo, -ĕre, go.
vădum, -i, *n.*, ford, shallows.
văgor, -ari, -atus, wander.
vălens, -tis, powerful, strong.
văleo, -ēre, -ui, -ĭtum, be strong,
have power.
vălĭdus, -a, -um, strong.
vallis, -is, *f.*, valley.
vānus, -a, -um, empty, insubstantial.
văpor, -ōris, *m.*, heat.
vărius, -a, -um, various; multi-
coloured.
vastus, -a, -um, huge.
vātēs, -is, *m.*, seer.
vĕho, -ĕre, vexi, vectum, carry,
bear; *(pass.)* ride, sail.
vēlāmen, -ĭnis, *n.*, covering, garment.
vellus, -ĕris, *n.*, skin, hide.
vēlo, -are, -āvi, -ātum, cover, wrap.
vēlox, -ōcis, swift.
vēlum, -i, *n.*, sail.
vĕlut, vĕlŭtĭ, as if, as.
vēna, -ae, *f.*, vein.
vēnātus, -ūs, *m.*, hunting, the chase.
vĕnēnĭfer, -ĕra, -ĕrum, poisonous.
vĕnēnum, -i, *n.*, poison.
vĕnia, -ae, *f.*, pardon.
vĕnio, -ire, vēni, ventum, come
vēnor, -əri, -atus, hunt.
ventus, -i, *m.*, wind.
Vĕnus, -ĕris, *f.*, (goddess of) love.
verber, -ĕris, *n.*, beating, stroke.
verbum, -i, *n.*, word.
vēro, but; indeed.
verto, -ĕre, -ti, -sum, turn, change.
vērus, -a, -um, true, genuine.
vestīgium, -i, *n.*, footprint.

vestīgo, -are, -āvi, -ātum, follow
the track of.
vestis, -is, *f.*, garment.
vĕto, -are, -ui, -ĭtum, forbid.
vĕtus, -ĕris, old.
via, -ae, *f.*, way, road; journey.
vibro, -are, -āvi, -ātum, brandish;
quiver; gleam.
victor, -ōris, *m.*, conqueror; *(adj.)*
victorious.
victōria, -ae, *f.*, victory.
vĭdeo, -ēre, vīdi, vīsum, see;
(pass.) appear, seem.
vĭgil, -ĭlis, wakeful.
vīginti, twenty.
vĭgor, -ōris, *m.*, strength.
villus, -i, *m.*, shaggy hair.
vīmen, -ĭnis, *n.*, twig, shoot; osier.
vincio, -ire, vinxi, vinctum, bind.
vinco, -ĕre, vīci, victum, conquer.
vincŭlum (vinclum), -i, *n.*, fetter,
fastening, lace.
vīnum, -i, *n.*, wine.
vĭŏlentus, -a, -um, violent.
vĭŏlo, -are, -āvi, -ātum, pollute,
violate, injure.
vīpĕreus, -a, -um, of a serpent.
vĭr, vĭri, *m.*, man; hero.
virga, -ae, *f.*, twig.
virgĭneus, -a, -um, girlish.
virgĭnĭtas, -atis, *f.*, virginity.
vĭrĭdis, -e, green.
vĭrīlis, -e, of a man, manly.
vīs, vim, vi, *f.*, force, violence;
(pl.) strength.
vīta, -ae, *f.*, life.
vĭtio, -are, -āvi, -ātum, taint, corrupt.
vīto, -are, -āvi, -ātum, shun; seek
to escape.
vīvax, -ācis, long-lived; lively.
vīvo, -ĕre, vixi, victum, live.
vīvus, -a, -um, living; natural.
vix, scarcely, with difficulty.
vōcālis, -e, vocal, melodious.
vŏco, -are, -āvi, -ātum, call, name,
summon.
vŏlo, velle, volui, wish.
vŏlūbĭlis, -e, circling, rolling.
vŏlucris, -is, *f.*, bird.
vŏluptās, -ātis, *f.*, enjoyment,
pleasure.

vōtum, -i, *n.*,   prayer, vow.
vox, vŏcis, *f.*,   voice.
vulgus, -i, *n.*,   common people
vulnus, -ĕris, *n.*,   wound.
vultus, -ūs, *m.*,   countenance.